Desolate No More

Recovering From the Ruins of a Broken Life:

The Beginning

Lisa M. Banks

ISBN:0692247521
ISBN-13: 978-0692247525

Note: This is my journey, so the actual names of the people
involved have been changed to protect their privacy

DEDICATION

This book is dedicated to my husband and children who are reminders of God's awesome love toward me. I would also like to give a special thanks to the spiritual leaders/mentors who were instrumental in my transformation process.

CONTENTS

AUTHOR'S NOTE

This is the first part of my journey. I wasn't able to put everything into one book, so I decided to start with the beginning where all the pain came from. The books to follow will contain the effects and challenges I faced from my painful start. I choose to do it this way in order for the reader to capture the full essence of my healing and transformation process. For most of my youth I felt as if I was nobody and would die young. I was a victim of sexual abuse, drug abuse, rape, and prostitution before the age of 19. Every negative experience caused me to sink deeper into the abyss of silence. I lived with fear and guilt as if everything that happened to me was my fault, no place for a young girl to abide. I was hurting but no one knew the turmoil within, they only saw anger and rebellion. Living this way even after accepting Christ into my life made me wonder if I was destined to nothing but painful reminders that I was a prisoner of my past. It wasn't until the Holy Spirit took me through the difficult process of healing that I began to see my life was more than my broken past. The journey wasn't easy but I had to release the prisoner within. The road to discovering the real person I buried deep within me in order to protect her actually showed me how underdeveloped I'd become. I was unable to connect with anyone, even myself! I was left with a challenge: Do I want to live or continue to be a victim? As the real me came to the surface I was able to find my voice. It felt so good to start talking about those things hidden inside of me. I've heard somewhere, "you're only as sick as your secrets." I didn't want to be sick anymore. I never realized how inhibited the pain kept me until I began to open up and allow God to bring the healing I needed. Now I want everyone to hear my story, not because I want to tell all of my business. It's to help those who are still prisoners of their past to know they don't have to serve a life sentence!

·

·

1
INNOCENCE LOST

When I shared my story for the first time publicly, it was in church. Other than my voice, you could hear a pin drop. The audience seemed captivated by my journey which gave me courage to keep talking. My niece happened to be in the audience that day and sat in the front row crying. I felt the strong temptation to throw the mic down and embrace her. I wanted to weep with her. She's my only niece and I thought either she was crying because she too had experienced terrible things or she felt bad because her aunt had. As I looked across the audience, I realized my niece wasn't the only one crying. I saw men, women, and teens with tears streaming down their faces. As I closed with my final sentence, I handed the mic over to my husband and went directly to my niece and cried with her. Looking up, I saw a sea of people at the church altar kneeling down with their heads in their hands. Sounds of people sobbing along with the voices of ministers praying filled the room. How could my story create a response like this? The feelings of shame and fear, that gripped me for all these years, were finally gone. My life, everything I had gone through, was now like an open book and shared with many. The fear and anxiety were no longer there; I was feeling lighter. There was a time when I felt nothing but shame when I thought of my past, but now I'm able to say I have history, but history doesn't have me.

There is a story in the Bible about a young girl named Tamar being raped by her half-brother Amnon. Tamar's oldest brother, Absalom, told her to keep quiet about the incident and not to take the matter to heart. What a thing to say to someone who has been violated. Unless you've been violated, being told not to take what happened to heart is impossible. Imagine how she felt after being attacked by her half-brother then having to keep quiet about it. The Bible says she lived as a desolate woman after this experience (2 Samuel 13). The Old Testament is written in the Hebrew language; the word *desolate* used to describe Tamar means ruined, devastated, or destroyed. When I first read this, I couldn't believe the Bible would have this type of content. Who would have thought that even the Bible talks about being violated and the effects of it? I believe Tamar, like any other young girl, had hopes and dreams, but could no longer find the desire to chase them after her experience. Tamar became a prisoner to the pain and torment of shame which comes from such an act. How would I know what Tamar felt since the Bible doesn't speak any more about this woman? I know because I was like Tamar, a girl full of hopes and dreams, but lost my innocence to the harsh realities of life. These harsh realities left me desolate.

As a child, I kept quiet like Tamar, not telling a soul about the terrible things that were happening to me and feeling powerless to stop them. The story of Tamar, found only once in the Bible, impacted the way I thought about how my own experiences affected my life. I was determined to not allow my story to end like Tamar's. I knew my story would be hard to tell, but I would not be silenced anymore, my voice would be heard.

For many years I hid all of my painful experiences within my heart. I kept them close, hurting others to numb the pain, but I didn't know that doing so would cause me to become a prisoner to the pain I tried to hide. I was tormented for many years, wishing God would kill me so I would no longer have to face myself in the mirror. I don't have external scars to remind me of what I've been through; I wish it could be that simple. The type of scars I had were internal, the kind no one could see at first. However, if you spent enough time with me you would eventually experience the scars of abandonment, rejection, and fear that were deep within.

My first childhood memory was finding a hiding place under the kitchen table. This table wasn't in the middle of the floor; it was up against the wall so it looked more like a cave to hide in. It was a small place of safety to the adult eye, but for a three-year-old it was the only place to quickly hide in the kitchen. I fought the urge to urinate—a sensation I would experience whenever I was afraid—uttering the words, "I'm sorry, I'm sorry, I didn't mean it." I really don't remember what happened after saying those words. I only recall what compelled me to hide. I called my mother the "B" word and the look she gave when I said that made me fear for my life. I was a bit confused at why she looked at me so harshly since that word, amongst other bad language, was used often in our household. What was wrong with me using a word I thought was normal for people to use in communicating while angry? I was angry with my mom so I could only do what I saw modeled. I'm not sure if she pulled me out or what, but all I remember is running under the table. Our relationship was never the same after this incident. She was no longer a safe place for me.

I grew up on the east side of Detroit with three brothers. My parents' marriage was rocky so there were times when my father would move out for a while. Whenever my father would drink there was always a fear that he would get into a fight with my mom. These fights wouldn't only be verbal, there were times it ended up physical. It was hard to watch the man who was my hero become this monster whenever intoxicated. I don't have a lot of memories of my father doing anything special for me that would make me see him as my hero other than protecting me from my older brother. My oldest brother and I would fight all the time over silly stuff; he would bump or mock me and I would use my spitfire tongue to lash out at him. My brother would get upset and resort to hitting me. If my dad was around, I would scream at the top of my lungs and he would come to my rescue. The only problem is my father wouldn't talk with my brother concerning the situation. Instead he would beat his behind with a wooden paddle, sometimes the beatings got out of control. Back then I felt like my brother deserved those beatings and I felt as if my father cared for me when he did this. Those beatings would get my mother riled up, not only causing more tension between my parents, but also between my brother and me. My mother would get so upset with me and had no problem letting me know she did not approve of what happened. However, her attitude and lack of understanding on my part caused me to think my mother only liked her sons. I do recall once being told by my mother, while she was angry with me, how she wished I was a boy and how it made me feel to hear her say that. Was it because my mother resented my father for all of the hurt she experienced with him, causing her to resent me when he came to my rescue? In my eyes, back then my father did no wrong and when he would hit my mother, I actually felt like she deserved it since, to me, she picked her sons over me. I needed someone to make me feel safe and during my younger years my dad filled that role.

One evening someone slipped something in my father's drink and he came home and tried to throw my mother out of the window. The next thing I knew my dad's sister and her husband came over and prayed for my dad. I remember him lying on the floor snarling and screaming while my oldest brother and I stood there and watched. I was around 10 years old at the time. We had two younger brothers, but I don't recall if they witnessed this. I saw my aunt give my dad a Bible and praying over him while he was still yelling. Then the most amazing thing happened after that. My dad got quiet. After a few seconds, he sat up and asked them what was going on. He didn't recall anything they told him he did, but became very remorseful. That day was the last time I saw my father drunk as a youth. He started going to prayer meetings after that. I think by then my mom had positioned herself to only be in the marriage for the sake of the children. She never went to any of the prayer meetings with my dad, but I did a couple of times.

In our house we had a den, which was my bedroom at the time. The den became my father's after that night and I was sent upstairs to the attic with my brother. By now my brother and I were older and whenever we fought we picked weapons ranging from hangers to knives. I stopped running to my dad for help because there were times when my brother would threaten to kill himself when he got beat. Though I hated that my brother would mess with me, I didn't want him to die so we fought it out. The next time my father got involved when we fought was when my brother burned me with an iron on my forearm. I screamed and my dad woke up to me holding my arm crying. He told me to put it under cold water and went after my brother for an explanation. I didn't go to the hospital since the lady down the street was a nurse and she tended to what she called a third-degree burn.

I don't really have a lot of good memories growing up, not because there weren't any, but because the bad outweighed the good. When I think of my childhood, the majority of my thoughts are traumatizing moments of fear, shame, abandonment, hate, and loneliness.

For a good portion of my youth I was molested, not just by one person, but also by strangers, a relative, and a friend of the family. I never told anyone I was being touched inappropriately since the name calling incident with my mom which left me running under the kitchen table. I adopted a thought pattern that even when doing something you don't know is wrong, a punishment was still right around the corner. For all I knew what was happening to me was my fault so in order to not get in trouble I thought it was better left unsaid. I was never told to not let anyone touch me, it felt wrong but simultaneously it gave me sensations that felt good. Not that my mom knew or understood the impact of that moment I ran under the table, she was only doing what she knew best. It's amazing how a response can change a relationship. As a parent, I now realized one wrong unresolved moment in anyone of my children's lives can make me a "no fly zone" for them futuristically. I longed for a relationship with my mother, however, it never came about until I was an adult and understood what happened during the earlier years of my life.

I remember the first time being molested. I was in kindergarten and he was a teenage boy who lived around the corner. He told me he had a doll for me. Being a gullible five-year-old, I went with him. He led me to his house into a bedroom I believe was his, since it didn't have any girly things around. He began to touch me in areas no one ever touched me before. Confused, I began to ask him about the doll he had for me. He told me when he was done he would get it for me. I asked him what he was doing and he told me we were playing house, and that he would beat me up if I told anyone we did this. When he was done, he took me into his sister's room and handed me one of her dolls. His sister and I were friends so I knew she would be upset with me for having her favorite doll. I told him this and he assured me he would tell her it was lost and not to worry. I left the house confused about what had happened and afraid he would beat me up if I told. I went home with the doll in my hand and headed straight to my room. A few hours later, his sister, my friend, came to the door upset because her brother told her I stole her doll. Dumbfounded, I gave her the doll and tried to explain that her brother gave it to me. When she asked why he would give me her doll nothing came out of my mouth. Should I risk telling her the doll was given because her brother pulled my pants down and touched me and told me he would beat me up if I told? My mother was standing there too and I didn't know what she would do. If I exposed how I really got the doll, would that get me in trouble with my mom? For a brief moment, time stood still in my mind as I battled with the thought of telling, but in the end I remained silent. My friend took her doll and never spoke to me again. From that moment on, I was never the same. I had become ashamed, a feeling that would keep me captive for years. My mother was angry with me for taking something that didn't belong to me. She just couldn't be trusted with the truth since I was ashamed to tell it. I was five years old and experienced something which gave me sensations I've never felt before, but didn't tell a soul. He never approached me again after that day. He didn't have to since there would be others who would take advantage of me instead.

There were times the molestations would happen in the middle of the night while I was upstairs in my bedroom and everyone else was downstairs sleeping. I remember some mornings waking up with my underwear rolled down to my knees and my shirt nicely rolled up over my chest. I didn't know what to think of it, since I had no memory of waking up in the middle of the night. It would happen periodically, so I just brushed it off as maybe I subconsciously had to use the bathroom in my sleep.

It wasn't until I was 17 years old while sleeping on the couch at my father's house that I found out I wasn't moving my clothes after all. My father wasn't home at the time and a relative happened to be over. I don't know about anyone else, but right before opening my eyes from a sleep, my senses are active, like hearing the television or feeling the blanket off of your feet. That's when I felt my shirt being rolled up and this person taking advantage of me while thinking I was asleep. I kept my eyes closed, afraid to open them as not to let him know I was awake. After a few minutes of him fondling my breasts, I felt my shirt being rolled down and he left out the front door. I almost threw up. I couldn't believe what had happened. The memories of me waking up with my shirt rolled up flooded my mind. I realized it wasn't me, it was him. I never told anyone about this incident until many years later, but only to my husband.

This wasn't the only person who would take advantage of my bedroom being upstairs away from everyone. Another male would come into my room, but he would wake me up. He'd have his way and then go into my brother's room to sleep. In order to get to my brother's room, you had to walk through mine, a move that caused us to fight at times. My brother would come upstairs long after I went to bed which would annoy me since he had to turn on my light and along with the noise of walking up the stairs, it would startle me out of my sleep. He also liked to leave the television on all night. I needed total silence to sleep so I would yell at him to turn the volume down. Needless to say, I won. My brother began to sleep on the living room sofa and I ended up with the entire upstairs to myself. Though I felt like I had won that war with my brother the battles of being touched in my sleep or awakened to be molested left me feeling utterly defeated. I don't know if anyone acknowledged the red flags when this guy (my brother's friend from down the street) wanted to sleep in the bedroom my brother abandoned. It was interesting why no one wondered why this guy would make his way upstairs going through the room of the only girl in the house. I hated this person, he did things to me the other's didn't do. He would orally stimulate me, but I had no idea what he was doing. It felt pleasurable, but wrong. I learned how to escape those moments with him. I would close my eyes and think I was somewhere else, anywhere but the present. Some nights he would try to make me orally stimulate him. Each time I refused. I was growing tired of being awakened by him, so one night I decided to say no. I felt such a hatred toward him it gave me courage to put an end to it. One night when he made his way through my room his pit stops ended with me acting as if I didn't want to wake up and I turned my back to him. He didn't stay upstairs; he walked back down and never came back up again. Actually he stopped staying overnight at my house after I did that. This guy ended up passing away at a young age, which after his death I told my mother he touched me whenever he stayed the night at our house. However, I didn't tell her until I was an adult.

I could not understand why this kept happening to me or the necessity to say something to an adult. I was unaware how these moments would shape my thoughts toward sex and the male gender. I didn't know sex was something special between a man and woman since I don't recall either of my parents sitting me or my siblings down to talk about our bodies or sex. The evidence of my ignorance pertaining to sex became quite clear when I reached high school. I didn't know what a virgin was until my boyfriend, who was a senior, asked if I was a virgin. I of course asked him what he meant by a virgin, so he said a person who hasn't had sex. I told him that I was indeed a virgin but would not have sex with him, he broke up with me.

Was I a virgin? Though I wasn't penetrated, one of the definitions of a *virgin* is unused, uncultivated, and unexplored. By that meaning alone, I was counted out. I was no longer virgin territory; areas of me had been explored and awakened long before they should have. There were feelings and sensations I felt that I didn't know how to properly digest. The once extroverted girl became a quiet, fearful, and numb shell. I kept all those moments locked inside afraid to tell anyone as if it were my fault this was happening. I recall the most intimate conversation my mother and I had about my body, she thought it was about the time I would begin my menstrual cycle. She gave me some sanitary napkins and told me that I will begin to bleed so I will need to use the pads to absorb the blood. She never explained how I would begin to ovulate and the possibility of getting pregnant if I were to have sex.

I had a love/hate relationship with those moments of being molested. Though I would close my eyes to escape the person who was doing this to me, I was feeling sensations, at first pleasurable, but it always left me consumed with shame and guilt afterward. I resented being a girl and wondered if I were a boy would this still happen. I didn't know how valuable my body was at the time since it had become a playground for some. I hear about purity workshops being done for our youth today and wonder how purity is only defined by being a virgin. I was a virgin in theory, but the purity of who I was, was violated years ago. Being pure doesn't mean you're not having sex; it's about who you are not just what you do. The heart and mind can become tainted with impure thoughts and desires creating a platform to act them out. The purity of my mind and heart was lost the first time I was touched. I had seen and felt things that transitioned me from a pure way of thinking about my body to almost longing for someone to touch me.

The older I got, the more I wanted to seek ways to have the sensations I felt fulfilled instead of having someone take advantage of me. I wonder about what caused my molesters to touch me and if they had been molested since some say that those who have been molested, end up molesting. Why would someone who knows the shame of what is being done to them do that to someone else? It's the issue of having some areas of your body awakened to feelings and urges you're unable to control so you begin to look to have them fulfilled. Sometimes there may not be someone around you who can mutually stimulate you so you find a person who can. I recall one time being at a neighbor's house and trying to touch a boy who was about a year or two younger than me. My intention was to fulfill an urge within me by reenacting with this boy what was done to me. I was unaware of how this boy would take what was being done to him, but heck by now I was used to this feeling and was beginning to enjoy the sensation. It was a failed operation since his mother opened the door to see what we were doing. She didn't catch us doing anything since by then we were done, however I didn't like coaching this boy to do what I wanted him to do. It was too much work for me. I think because doing that made me have to be the aggressor, something I wasn't comfortable with, so I never did that again. This was the foundation of my sex education, though I watched the sex education videos in middle school. I had hands on experience and now years later see the destructive path it put me on. I didn't learn until well into my adulthood the impact those years had on my ability to be intimate. I was craving intimacy and wanted someone to touch my soul the way my body was touched. I learned how to live without connecting, even with myself. Little did I know how my life would continue to spiral into a dark abyss of sex, drugs, alcohol, and homelessness to the point where death looked like the only way out. This would all happen to me before my twentieth birthday.

2
LEARNING TO MEDICATE THE PAIN

Although I carried the burden of my experiences, there was a sense of worth I found in going to school. I could lose myself in my friends and homework. While in elementary school I would write stories and the teacher would allow me to share them with the class. I found myself becoming the teacher's pet in most of my classes, a position I enjoyed immensely. I was a smart young girl who loved to learn and write. I would write poems and songs at home and on weekend mornings I would wake up early to sing them so no one would hear me. Though I was intelligent, it was quite clear I had pain growing inside of me since my stories would involve a young girl who was angry. These stories would make the other kids laugh and gave me the attention I longed for. Looking back I see how those stories were really my cries of what was going on deep within me which I could not verbalize.

In middle school I would come home, go to my room, turn on the radio, and listen to it for hours. Losing myself in music allowed me to avoid thinking of what was around me. I stopped writing during my teenage years. It was hard for me to put into words what was going on inside of me. I was turning inward to find relief from my pain, barricading myself from the world in order to survive my experiences. One night confirmed my reasoning to internalize my feelings. I had a tape recorder once and used it to tape myself singing some of the songs I would write. These were songs of pain; songs of longing for someone to rescue me from the world I lived in. My mother took my tape recorder and in front of company played one of the songs I taped of myself singing. The snickering that took place from my mother and those who could hear made me embarrassed and shameful. Already struggling with shame from the molestations, I made a vow to not allow what was within me to come out anymore. I know my mother had no idea what that did to me, nor do I blame her for causing me to close in. She may have thought what happened was cute, but I had no filters to help me understand anything positive, I only saw things as a negative when people did things for me or to me. I found safety in music which helped me escape from reality but I no longer wrote music or poems. My dreams of being on stage singing and visualizing an audience applauding my performances would begin to take a back seat. Being in my room for hours lost in the fantasy of being someone else because I hated myself was not enough anymore. Music was the first thing I found to rescue me, but it wouldn't be the last. I would soon find other things to keep me from the reality of my nothingness.

While in the seventh grade I enjoyed my first joint. I

remember being at a friend's house skipping school, smoking marijuana and playing Pac-man. I found getting high helped me feel numb—something music didn't do. Being high made everything so calm with no thoughts of my life whereas music would cause me to feel. I was tired of feelings. When I was high I was relaxed and didn't have a care in the world. Not being able to think or feel was what I needed from my lonely world of torment.

My body was well developed during the seventh grade, so I started dressing in tight jeans hoping one of the cute boys would pay attention to me. Though I did struggle with what people thought of me, it didn't help that I developed breasts earlier than my peers. They thought I stuffed my bra and accused me publicly of doing so. The boys started grabbing my breasts and yelled out that they felt real. No matter how many boys would do it there was always someone reaching toward my chest. Though I felt humiliated, I actually liked the attention.

There was a time in eighth grade while walking with my cousin and a couple of friends, a group of boys began to tease one of the girls. She didn't respond and I took the liberty of telling them to leave her alone. I knew some of the boys from having the same class so I felt somewhat comfortable standing up for her. The next thing I knew, they started picking on me and talking about my body, and they started reaching for my chest and butt. I pushed them away and told them to stop all while walking backwards trying to protect myself. I was also hoping for someone from the group to tell them to leave me alone. That didn't happen and suddenly I found myself backed up against a house crouching down in a fetal position because they overpowered me. I tried to cover my breasts the best I could but their hands were all over me. I screamed for help with hope that someone would come to my rescue. I was so scared and began to cry. The next thing I heard was a male voice yelling out to leave me alone and feeling fewer hands touching me. I looked up and saw a guy with a stick hitting the boys off me. He helped me up and told my friends to make sure to take me home and tell my parents. He watched as I walked away with my cousin and friends. I asked the girls I was with why didn't they help me and their reply was they were afraid. I believe they were afraid because we were a group of white girls and the group of boys who attacked me were black. When I told my mother, she informed the school and the boys whom I could identify were punished. I don't remember what their punishment was, but I finally felt like my mother cared for me. My father who figuratively was my refuge at the time wasn't the one who was there that day, it was my mom.

After that day I always looked down in order to prevent eye contact with anyone for fear something like that would happen again. I did not speak up to anyone about anything unless pushed into a corner, and then everything would just come out. I was a spitfire when provoked, but it would take a lot to get me to do it.

Eighth grade was when I started drinking at parties held by relatives; I would take sips from my parents' glasses. I enjoyed the feeling alcohol gave me, a feeling of power and boldness. My parents never really said anything to me since they were present during the parties. This was another thing to add to my list of prescriptions when I needed to feel better. The list kept growing. Not too much later, I had started to smoke cigarettes regularly and found it quite cool and relaxing. I learned how to blow circles when I exhaled and that made me look even cooler. Of course I was too young to have a job to support my newly found habit so I would take cigarettes from my parents and go upstairs to my room to smoke.

Also during this time I figured my parents didn't really care where I went since I was able to do and go anywhere I wanted. I don't recall seeking permission from my mother to walk the streets of Detroit. I loved walking; it gave me time to daydream and another way for me to medicate myself. I would dream about being someone better than me and someplace different. I also found while walking guys would drive by blowing their horn or whistling at me. I craved attention and sometimes guys would stop and ask if I needed a ride but I had enough sense to say no. I was falling in love with the attention my looks got. No one had to touch me; all I wanted was someone to tell me I was pretty.

Positive affirmations seemed to only come from outside my home. I felt like a nobody and if I came up missing I wouldn't be missed. I believe that's why I started running away from home, even though I would only go around the neighborhood. There was a hope to hear that my mother was looking for me and wanted me back. I only had a few places to go, so each time my mother would come and get me. I didn't communicate any of my feelings to anyone, because I didn't know how to connect with my emotions. I felt like a shell, nothing inside, only a hard exterior that prevented anyone from getting close. So I would only act out what was going on in me.

I grew more distant from my family each year and it began to reflect in my music choices. I would listen to songs that talked about being hurt or being alone. My favorite song while in eighth grade was, "I Don't Care Anymore" by Phil Collins which came out in 1982. This song was everything I demonstrated in my behaviors, but not capable to say. It became my anthem for many years. I see now how the song justified my actions for keeping people at a distance. I wanted to care, but because of the things that happened to me, I only became cold and callused. When I listen to the song now, it hurts my heart knowing how much I was a ticking time bomb waiting to go off at any minute.

There was a voice screaming so loudly on the inside, but no one could hear it but me. No one knew how to reach me because I wouldn't let them in. Shame had imprisoned me. All the years of being touched and mishandled caused me to shrink back into myself.

The molestations were not as frequent during my teen years since they only happened when I was home. Knowing this, I spent a lot of my time away. Spending many nights at friends or a cousin's house helped me find some sense of normalcy. By the summer of 1983, my middle school friendships would end for me as we were starting high school and began to go our separate ways. Although many of them stayed in touch during those years, I ended up not being in their circle. That's when things became more complicated.

In my sophomore year, I lost my virginity. I dated a guy who I thought really liked me. When I finally gave in and had sex with him, he totally lost interest. This was the guy I thought I would share my life with. He was the first one to tell me he loved me. How could I not believe it, he called me all the time and would spend every free moment with me. He bought me jewelry, flowers, and took me to the show. He wooed me. When I was with him the world seemed so much better, until we had sex. I didn't even know how precious my virginity was, let alone the possibilities of getting pregnant. A couple of months after our first time, he started to give me the cold shoulder. I was devastated; this guy was everything to me. He was the first person I let in my heart and I didn't understand how he could do this to me. He would lie and cheat, and at first I was in denial, but after a few months of bad treatment, I finally gathered enough courage to break up with him. I was tired of getting hurt. He didn't take the break-up well but I had enough. Shortly after breaking up with him, I missed my monthly cycle. I told my mom and she asked if I was having sex. When I told her yes, she was livid. I just sat there wondering how was I to know not to have sex. She never told me not to have sex so I had no idea why she would be mad. I felt like I was under the kitchen table again. I felt ashamed and after a few choice words from her, she took me to the doctor and it was confirmed, I was pregnant. That was a tough blow. Immediately, my mom scheduled an appointment to have an abortion. I was 15 years old and having an abortion. It was a surreal moment for me. Heck, I didn't know the physical dangers of having an abortion or the psychological impact that decision would have on me.

We arrived at a small clinic with a sign that read "Family Planning" and I watched my mother fill out a clipboard with several pages attached to it. When my name was called to come to the back, I went without realizing what happened next would haunt me. After changing into a gown, I was asked to lay on what looked like a hospital bed and relax. The doctor came in and began to explain what would happen. He explained how a tube would be put inside of me and would basically suck out the baby in small pieces. He told me I could hold the nurse's hand during this time and to squeeze her hand if it hurt. I was given something to relax me more and then the procedure started. I remember watching the pieces of what was within me go through the the tube. It hurt like crazy; my stomach was cramping so bad tears streamed down my eyes. The doctor told me to hang in for a while longer and it would be over. I never forgot about the baby who lived inside of me for such a brief time. I had the abortion early December 1984. I remember because when Christmas came all I got was a curling iron. My mom reminded me she had to spend money on the abortion and for me to consider it as part of my Christmas gift. I was devastated. I remember going to my room crying and thinking how I hated my life.

Little did my parents know, I struggled with thoughts of setting the house on fire while everyone was fast asleep and watch them go up in flames. I wanted to hurt my family because I was hurting. To be young, full of pain and tormented with thoughts of murder is something no teenager should have to experience. I'm sure there are many more who are suffering like I was, silently screaming for help and no one hearing them. I found being under the influence of drugs or alcohol allowed me to forget about the anger within me, so I would get wasted every chance I could. Being intoxicated made me feel stronger and bolder, something I lacked while sober. Though I felt stronger and bolder, it was expressed so negatively. I used my sharp tongue which would spit out words that hurt more than any hit. I was angry at everyone because I felt like I'd been dealt a terrible hand and it was me against the world.

I was hurting and wanted the pain to go away. In order to avoid the painful memories of the abortion, I sought comfort with another guy who also was an enemy of the boy who impregnated me. This guy was different though. He didn't cheat on me or lie to me, even after having sex with him. He did the exact opposite, wanting to spend time together because, like me, he was hurting too. His mother left them and his father allowed him and his brother to do whatever they wanted. My parents would let me stay the night over his house and he introduced me to a different drug to use, heroin. We didn't inject it; we smoked it using a bong. This high was nothing like weed or alcohol. My heart started racing and I could not catch my breath. I thought I was going to die. The room felt like it was closing in on me and I didn't like that at all. I coughed for quite some time after my first inhale. Needless to say, I never tried that again.

During that time I got kicked out of school because the guy who got me pregnant found out I had an abortion and was now sleeping with his enemy. He had his family tell the superintendant that I didn't live in the district. I was called down to the superintendant's office and he told me that since I didn't live in the district, in order for me to stay for the remainder of the 1985 school year, my family had to pay $400.00. My heart dropped, I had just had an abortion and got nothing for Christmas, how could I talk my mom into paying more money for me to go to school? I knew she wouldn't do it, so I just got up and walked out of the office thinking how my life was nothing but pain and disappointment. I was hurt; school was one of my methods of escape. My English teacher went down to the office trying to fight for me to stay, but it wasn't enough. I had to say goodbye to Hamtramck High School and the friends I made there.

I still hung out in Hamtramck with my new boyfriend. Our relationship consisted of having sex, doing drugs and drinking alcohol while listening to rock and roll. All of the things I needed to get away from the world around me were now within my reach. This guy was just as messed up as I was. What I didn't know was he had a hidden addiction that would soon cause us to split up. We would sit and listen to Led Zeppelin, AC/DC, or any hard rock band while smoking joints laced with cocaine. At the time, I thought this was so cool and amazing. I don't remember most of what we did other than getting high and having sex. This time I thought I was a little smarter and used condoms for protection. Though my mother supported me using birth control pills since the abortion, I had a hard time remembering to take them. I would stay nights at my boyfriend's house and it may have appeared my freedom was fun and exciting to those whom I hung around with, but it carried a painful price.

One night when my father picked me up from hanging out in Hamtramck, my pants (which were very tight) ripped while waiting for him. When we got home, I told my parents about my pants, but they only noticed I was higher than a kite. My parents began to tell me how I seemed to keep making bad choices in boyfriends and how this guy wasn't any better than the last. We went back and forth arguing about my current flame when my oldest brother came in to give his two cents. I don't remember what he said, all I recall is getting up and grabbing a knife and going after him with it. I wanted to hurt my brother and I finally had the chance to do it. I hated him for all the years of picking on me, slapping me in front of his friends, and tearing down the posters of my favorite rock bands from my bedroom walls. I had all this anger in me and he was about to feel it. Both of my parents struggled to restrain me from stabbing him. Finally they knocked the knife from my hands and watched me drop to my knees. I started banging my fists into the chair screaming at the top of my lungs of how much I hated everybody and I wanted to kill my brother. I ranted and raved until I was exhausted. Without knowing what to do, my parents just sent me to my room.

Rage boiled up inside of me waiting for an opportunity to be released, and that was one of those times when I felt out of control. I suppressed my emotions because I was unable to manage them. That wasn't the only time when my uncontrolled emotions got me in trouble. One time my mother was expressing how she wanted to have a relationship with me and how much she loved me. All I could do was laugh. My mother was insulted and angry and she walked away. She didn't know the real reason I laughed was because I was happy, but my ability to properly express feelings was twisted.

Not long after my night of defending my current boyfriend's love for me and mine for him, our relationship ended. I found out he was snorting cocaine which made him paranoid. He started accusing me of cheating on him and became verbally abusive toward me when I denied it. I hated that my parents were right, and they made sure to remind me of what a bad choice he was when I told them we split up.

After breaking up with him I thought maybe if I could

just have sex with a guy without getting involved in a relationship, no one would get their feelings hurt. I was tired of expecting someone to love me and unfortunately I thought having sex would bring that to me. I had to change my approach. I liked the feeling sex gave me, but hated the emotional pain of a broken relationship. I learned how to turn off my emotions, a practice I learned in the process of being sexually abused. As summer quickly approached I soon found out how emotionally detached I'd become.

3
WANDERING SOUL

My parents' marriage ended in divorce when I turned fifteen. My siblings and I stayed with my mom. I was very angry with her for splitting up with my dad as she was the one who wanted to end it. He moved in with family members a few miles away from us, so I was able to go visit him sometimes. My mom worked at a flea market on weekends so she helped me get a job at one of the other booths. She allowed me to smoke cigarettes in front of her, but wasn't willing to support my habit, so this was a way for me to buy my own cigarettes. My mom would take me to work every weekend and I believe she hoped we would develop a better relationship. It never happened since I had nothing but resentment toward my mother. Though she tried her best to reach out to me, it was an unsuccessful attempt since I was too far gone at that point. I was currently dealing with a habit of smoking weed daily along with whatever alcohol I could get my hands on.

During the week, my mom worked days. I found myself looking forward to her being gone so I could hang out in the streets. I spent most of my time hanging around the wrong crowd. My mother hated the people I was with, not knowing I was the one influencing some of the bad things we did. By the time my sixteenth birthday came around, my relationship with my mother was extremely rocky. I spent my birthday smoking weed, drinking Southern Comfort, and hanging with the neighborhood car thieves. I got high or drunk every day in order to function. The fantasy of killing my family by burning the house down still engulfed my mind. I began to start fires, playing out my fantasy without anyone getting hurt. I didn't understand it at the time, but that was another outward expression of my internal torment.

Because I internalized a lot of stuff, I never learned how to talk about my feelings. Heck, I didn't know how to handle my feelings, let alone explain how I felt. Getting high was the only way for me to not think anymore. I wanted to enjoy life so any means to stop being tormented by my thoughts would work. Although my thoughts would eventually catch up to me, I found getting high to be a temporary relief.

I became very promiscuous and had no standards. Really, I didn't know how to value myself. I started having sex with random guys. If they looked good to me, I wanted them. There were times I would just meet a guy and the next thing you know we would have sex. I wasn't looking for someone to buy me flowers or call me the morning after, I just wanted to have sex. It was like I couldn't control myself and I didn't want to. My mother would pull me out of cars and scream at me for sitting in a car with a grown man drinking and smoking pot. I would just look at her with such hatred. Keep in mind I was only 16 years old. I didn't see it as an act of love, only embarrassment and pain.

Partying was more important than going home so I ended up staying with the car thieves next door for a few weeks. I no longer rode with my mom to the flea market. I asked a couple of the guys I met there to pick me up. Unfortunately there was a hefty price to pay for those rides to work. One of the guys tried to get me to perform oral sex on him, but I refused. He was married and I did have one standard: you don't mess with married men. So his generosity to give me rides ended at that point. I asked another guy who wasn't married if he could start picking me up. His price was to see me topless and to touch me. You may not understand why I chose to let someone do that to me, but I was so numb that I didn't care. If doing that got me to where I needed to go, then I let him do whatever. I stopped asking him for rides after he told me he had a friend who took pictures of topless girls and would pay me if I posed for the man. I told him I wasn't interested in having pictures taken of me. I never told my mom about it, as she knew both of those guys, so I decided to stop working at the flea market after the second incident.

While hanging with the car thieves next door, I got into a fight with a girl who hit me so hard I lost consciousness. When I came to, blood was all over me from a busted nose in need of stitches. My parents came to the hospital to get me and it was decided that I would move in with my dad, who now lived with my cousin and her husband in a three-bedroom bungalow. The new school year had started and my mom enrolled me in Osborn High School. The school was near my dad's house but my mom would drive me there each morning. She watched me walk into the front door of the school not knowing that I walked out the back door to go back home. I hated going there. One of my cousins who went there really wasn't talking much to me anymore. Our relationship wasn't like it was when we were kids. She had a steady boyfriend and I was considered the loose girl. I also crossed racial lines, so that was a big deal within our family. It seemed as soon as my relatives learned I hung around black people, it was as if I became the black sheep of the family. So I was left again to myself. I struggled daily with thoughts of abandonment and rejection. It seemed like my life was full of pain and I didn't like it much at all. I contemplated suicide, but didn't go through with it. I was afraid to hurt myself or experience more pain than I was feeling, so why inflict more? I would take the bottle of rubbing alcohol and hold it to my mouth daring myself to gulp it all down. I had no idea the damage it would cause or if it would work, so I would put the cap back on and walk away. Deep down there was a girl who loved life and wanted to live, but remained trapped in the walls I built around to protect her from the pain. There were many nights I would cry myself to sleep thinking no one liked me, not even God.

It wasn't long before my cousin and her husband moved out. That left just my dad and me, but the cool thing was he rarely stayed home. This was like a great thing for me since I could do whatever I wanted. I officially dropped out of school and got high all day every day. What a life! I would wake up to a 40-ounce of beer and a pack of Newport cigarettes. I thought, 'This is awesome!' I didn't have a future, but I had a lot of history for someone just short of turning 17 years old. Without my dad being home, I had free roam of the house and streets. I had a few guys who would come pick me up just to have sex. This was about as close to having a relationship as I was willing to go. To tell you the truth, I didn't know their last names, where they lived, or if the first name they gave me was the real one.

I found myself in some scary situations because of my decisions to be so free with myself. There was a time when one guy wouldn't let me leave the house he took me to. It wouldn't have been a big deal had I not brought a friend with me this time and she was freaking out, crying and carrying on about how they were going to kill us. I kept a clear mind and waited for the right moment. The house was full of people, so we were put in a back room with a TV and were told we weren't going back home. The front door had a dead bolt on it so without the key it was useless. As the day progressed, someone went to the door to let the dog out, and that's when I saw my chance. I bolted for the door and pushed the person aside and ran out into the street. I stood in the middle of the street yelling, "Take me home now or I'm going to the police." In hindsight, why didn't I just go to the nearest telephone booth and call 911? Doing that got me home that day; unfortunately, my friend never spoke to me again since I put her in harm's way.

Living with my dad was great until he announced he had a girlfriend and she was coming to live with us. I wasn't very fond of her and she tried to win me over with drugs and alcohol. I would accept her gifts, but still didn't like her very much. One day while my dad was at work, his girlfriend said something to me that caused me to snap. I don't even remember what she said, but I recall running after her as she ran into the house and closed the screen door and locked it. I banged on the door telling her to open it so I could kill her. She was afraid of me and I knew it. I remembered we had a phone in the garage so I jumped the fence to the backyard to call my dad. I wanted him to tell her to let me in the house because it wasn't her house and I believed my dad would make her let me in. The opposite actually happened. He told me to find somewhere else to go. I couldn't believe my ears. Was he kicking me out or was he telling me to wait until he got home? I later found out that he was upset I'd threatened his girlfriend, and she felt like she couldn't live in the same house with me. So in a nutshell, I was put into the streets. I was enraged with my father's decision. The man who I sought refuge in, had abandoned me for another person. I couldn't believe it. I thought if I walked to my mother's home she would let me in and all would be well. Though my cousins lived down the street, I never thought of going to their house. I made the long walk to my mom's house. When I got there, my grandmother was babysitting my little brothers. She would not let me in since my mom wasn't home, so I asked if I could just come in and call my mom. She let me and I called my mom at work and asked if I could stay with her since my father kicked me out. She told me no. I recall yelling in the phone, 'What am I supposed to do?' since I had nowhere to go. I sat there and cried for a minute as I couldn't believe this was happening. I was used to being the one not coming home for days at a time—not being kicked out.

I remembered a guy gave me his number and told me if

I ever needed a place to go I could call him. When I called him to ask for help he came and picked me up. I only knew his first name and only met him once, but I had no one else to help me. He drove me to his house and had me hide in the closet since his mother wasn't fond of white people. I didn't care; it was a place to lay my head. The next day he drove me to his sister's house to let me hang out there. I slept on the hard wood floor of her living room that night. During those two days I hadn't eaten, so my stomach was pretty empty and the growling could be heard across the room. The guy I was with went to the store to buy me a bag of chips to eat. He ate breakfast with his sister and all I got was a bag of chips! I was upset since I felt like he should have thought of me, so I spoke up. This led into an argument and me leaving the house. I didn't know where I was going, but I was so upset I didn't care. I knew where I was, so I started walking toward my old neighborhood. As I walked from his house, I ran into a guy who offered me a beer. I was starving for anything so I drank it. The last time I was that hungry was when I ran away from home and saw a guy eating a whopper sandwich from Burger King and throwing away what he didn't finish. As soon as he walked away I ran to the garbage and ate it. This time there was no one eating around me, so I guess beer would have to do. We sat at his kitchen table drinking beer and making small talk. When we finished drinking, I thanked him and told him that I had to be on my way. Looking back I think how crazy that was. He could have hurt me. To this day I believe God was with me and keeping me even when making bad decisions.

Now tipsy from the beer, I walked past a phone booth

and thought maybe my mom would have let me come home since it had been a couple of days. Before I could pick up the phone to make a collect call, three guys were passing by and asked if I would like to get high with them. Those were magic words to my ears! The phone call could wait until later. So I went with the guys—I didn't know them nor did I ask what their names were. I wanted to get high. I ended up in a basement of a house smoking joints with three guys I'd just met. Who does that? As we completed one joint before another could be lit, I heard a small voice in my head tell me to get out. Suddenly a door opened and a young girl said something to one of the guys, which was my cue. I told them I had to go and thanked them for sharing their stash with me. They tried so hard to talk me into staying; I learned to listen to any nudging so I left. Back on the streets, I walked for a bit and started to feel weird. I don't know if it was what I smoked or if my lack of eating was causing the feeling. All I remember is feeling very strange after leaving that basement. I passed a school with a group of guys playing basketball. One of my brother's friends noticed me and began to call my name. I gazed across the busy street and saw him waving to me, so I decided to cross the four-lane road to get to him. When I got to the other side of the road the first words that came out of my mouth was how high I was and how good it was to see him. I began to tell him I had nowhere to go since both of my parents kicked me out. He told me he would take me somewhere so I could get some rest. I'm not sure whose house he took me to, but we were in a basement that had a pool table and there were people talking and drinking. Of course, I started drinking with them.

The next thing I remember was waking up face down

on the pool table. Some guy was waking me up telling me I could go home with him. Getting the go ahead from my brother's friend that the guy was safe, I left with him. I recall walking a few blocks from where we were. The neighborhood we walked through had only a few houses still standing on the block, the rest were torn down. We walked into a house that looked run down on the outside, however upon entering the home, it was well kept. He lived with his mother and little brother who were in a room watching television when we came in. I was directed to a bedroom where we could be alone. The next day when I woke up, he gave me something to eat and a towel to wash up with. He was very kind and told me he had to go to work but to wait for him to get back. I felt really awkward being in a house where I knew no one, not even the guy I came in with. I quietly tried to leave, but was stopped by his little brother asking me why I was leaving. He told me his brother told him I was staying until he came back home from work. I remember telling him I had somewhere to go and to make sure to thank him for letting me stay. I then turned away, walked out the door, and made my way into the streets once again.

I ended up back at my mother's home hoping she would have changed her mind. It had been a couple of days since I last asked so maybe she would help me after she found out I was still on the streets. Unfortunately, there was no welcome mat for me. My grandmother was there again watching my little brothers so I asked to use the phone to call my mom. I called my mom who told me I was not able to come back and that I should call my father. Instead of calling my father, I grabbed the Yellow Pages and found a place I thought would take me. When I called, the person on the other end told me my parents or guardian would have to release me to their care since I was under the age of 18. I told the person that wouldn't happen since both of my parents didn't want me in their home let alone take me somewhere. The conversation ended with, "I can't help you" from the voice on the other end. I hung up sobbing and thinking, 'Nobody wants me.' I sat there frozen because I didn't know what to do. I later called my mother at work and begged her to let me stay. She wouldn't let me stay, but she said she would call my dad since I shouldn't be in the streets.

I left my mother's home disappointed and feeling like I had nothing and no one. I walked back to my dad's neighborhood waiting for him to come home since I believed my mom would call him. I knew she was upset with him for kicking me out for so long because his girlfriend didn't want me to stay there. While walking back to my dad's, I met some people who asked me if I'd like to party with them. At that moment I totally forgot about the conversation I had with my mother, who was planning to call my dad. I cannot remember any of the names of the people or exactly how we connected. I accepted their invitation and we partied for a couple of days. There were times I would wake up lying on the floor. I didn't need to go find a home, I had a place to hang and party without any problems.

Everything was going well until a fight broke out. Everyone who didn't live there was kicked out into the streets. A few of us started walking around the neighborhood in the middle of the night laughing and drinking. As we walked, I saw a familiar face, a guy who lived down the street from my dad, who I'll call Leonard.

As we passed Leonard, he asked me to come to him. He asked me why I was hanging with them in the middle of the night. I told him I was kicked out and had no place to go, so he told me to leave them and he would take me somewhere. So I left with Leonard and went to his house. I didn't remember that my mom was supposed to call my dad to get me back in the house, until I woke up the next morning, so I decided to leave Leonard and go to my dad's house down the street. He let me inside with no mention of where I'd been or how I managed to live for that period of time. I just summed it up that whatever my mom said to him worked. His girlfriend wasn't happy. While I was gone, she gave my bedroom to her two children who also happened to move in while I was on the streets. I wasn't in any shape to fight so I just went to sleep in my new bedroom.

After my overnight stay with my neighbor, Leonard, he became what I would call a regular sex partner. He lived across the street from me and scared away any guy who would show up at my house. Being extremely dysfunctional, I thought that was his way of saying he liked me. That was not the case. He was crazy and I would soon find out.

My dad and his girlfriend finally broke up after I told how she was cheating on him, in his own house. I was so happy when she left, now I could have my old room back and do whatever I wanted. One night a guy I knew paid my cab fare to come visit him at his house. I went and found his invitation to not be so nice. When I arrived, the guy and his friend were in the basement, but he left to go upstairs to get something. The friend proceeded to make sexual advances toward me, which I refused. By rejecting his advances it resulted in him pulling up my dress trying to rape me. I screamed at the top of my lungs. Suddenly the upstairs door opened and the guy who invited me ran downstairs grabbed me and hit me. I screamed and tried to fight him back, this resulted in both of them calling me a bunch of names and kicking me out of the house. I had on a summer dress and flats so I was not prepared to walk all the way home. I was about six miles from my dad's house and it was in the middle of the night. I was a white girl walking the streets of Detroit alone. Can you say "vulnerable"? Cars would slow down or would stop several feet ahead of me. I was so scared. I went to a pay phone and dialed 911 hoping for some help, but all I got from the operator was instructions to walk to the next phone booth and call if anyone tried to assault me. I walked for about a mile when I realized my shoes were creating blisters on my feet. As I kept walking, a Mercedes Benz pulled up next to me with a black man and white woman inside. The woman, who was on the passenger's side, rolled down the window and asked me where such a young girl would be going in the middle of the night, I told them I was walking home and she told me to get in and that they would take me there. They introduced themselves to me as Mark and Nina. I got into the back seat and was relieved to get off of my feet since they were throbbing. What I didn't realize was that the couple who just picked me up was really a prostitute and her pimp. I should have known since it was in the wee hours of the morning and they were driving as if it was the middle of the day. I explained to the couple what happened and was afraid to go back home because I was locked out and didn't want to wake up my dad. They took me to their motel room so I could rest until I thought my dad would be awake and let me in. While in the motel, Mark asked if he could rub my blistered feet. Not refusing the pleasure of being pampered, I let him massage my feet. Nina began shooting up heroin between her toes and told me never to do drugs because it was a bad habit. She asked me if I ever worked the streets and I told her no. Nina told me to never start because there is nothing good in the streets. They drove me home that afternoon, however that wasn't the last time we would come together.

I became friends with this couple, and often talked with them. Mark had a day job as an electrician so she and I would drive around in his car from time to time. Though Nina told me not to start selling my body, she also asked me to do a favor. She had a trick (customer) who wanted a threesome. She told me I would make a nice amount of money for only a few minutes and she didn't trust anyone else to do it with her. I agreed and Nina ended up coaching me through my first experience of using my body for money. I felt very awkward, but it was the easiest way I'd earned money. I remember sitting in the motel room after she and the man left feeling like, 'Wow, did I just do that?'

A few days after that experience my uncle, who lived down the street, brought a friend over to my dad's house one evening. My uncle's friend was a person that I would call at the time, a 'Jesus Freak.' We talked about Jesus and how much He loves us. By the end of the conversation, I said the prayer of salvation. I actually remember feeling excited because this guy told me all my sins would be forgiven and that everything would be new. That was a good thing since I had done a lot wrong in my young life.

It was short lived since I went down the street to a friend's house and Leonard happened to be there upset. He was upset because he contracted a venereal disease and wanted to find someone to blame. At that point I hadn't had sex with anyone else other than with him and the threesome I was in didn't involve me having intercourse, so I knew it wasn't me. Leonard proceeded to try to embarrass me in front of those who were sitting on the porch with us with words like "white trash," "hoe." and "slut." I just sat there not knowing what to do since he was considered crazy. I say that because I remember walking with him one time and a guy ran up on us with a gun getting ready to shoot him. He took off running leaving me to be confronted by this guy carrying a pistol ready to pull the trigger. The guy didn't do anything to me. He said if I was Leonard's girlfriend I was stupid because he left me to get shot. Leonard apologized to me later, but it didn't take away the fact he left me. Now he was standing in front of me calling me names and accusing me of giving him a disease. He was the unfaithful one; he slept with anyone he could get a hold of, which made him vulnerable to disease. I could only stand there and tell him it wasn't me and the next thing I knew, a gun was pointed to my head. I knew this guy was serious, so I did what any person who had nothing to live for would do. I asked him to pull the trigger. Why not? I had nothing to lose or gain. I was not afraid to die. I had nothing to live for anyway. He put the gun away and told me I was stupid. Though he didn't pull the trigger, I felt like I was dying anyway. I went home after that, but I still messed around with him. His bad behaviors later caught up to him.

There were nights I would get so drunk or high in

order for me to fall asleep. One evening stands out to me, only because I was feeling lonely and unloved, so I prayed. I knew of God, but thought I had to be like the Catholic nuns who to me were holy and blameless, something I was not. I asked God to give me someone to love me like a baby and wouldn't leave me. I cried so hard that night. I was hurting and longed to connect with someone. I'm not saying God answered my prayer, but I will say I got pregnant shortly after that night. I was so excited until I had to tell my family and Leonard.

4
BABY'S HERE

When I broke the news of my pregnancy to my dad, he told me I would be keeping this one. Little did he know I wanted this baby. Finally, I would have someone who would love me no matter what. I was only 17 years old. I didn't think of what I had to offer this child. My only thought was what this baby would do for me. The ability to properly provide for this child was not within my means—no high school education and no hope for the future, only a desire to be loved. Did you hear my prayer to give me someone to love me, not someone for me to love? Did I want someone to love or someone who wouldn't leave me? Why would I think having a child would bring love into my life? I thought, 'God help this child who is coming into my world that's filled with hardness and pain, and me expecting love to be the outcome.'

My mother was the second person to get the news of my pregnancy, which didn't go well as you can imagine.

When she found out the father was black, she flipped. Her advice to me was to give the child up for adoption because no white man would ever want me if I had a black baby. My mother decided to stop talking to me at that point. At the time, I didn't care. I was getting what I wanted and she couldn't stop me. I was still living with my dad, who was in a serious relationship with another woman who happened to be black too. I liked his girlfriend; she was cool. She took on the role of a mother to me and helped me get prenatal care through a free clinic and took me to my first appointment. Everything was going well until I decided to tell Leonard. After talking to one of his family members, I found out he was in jail. When I finally spoke with him after accepting a collect call, the news of a baby didn't make him jump up and down with excitement. Instead, the first thing to come from his mouth was, "It's not mine." That did not sit well with me. I stopped talking to him after that statement. I didn't need him. He was in jail and couldn't do anything for me behind bars anyway. What could he do for a child? My life began to take a turn at this point. I was a couple months pregnant and believed I was getting what I prayed for—someone to love me. There seemed to be a hefty price to pay for this love to come my way. My mother ended up disowning me and the father was nothing but a donor. Did I think this through? I wanted someone to love me, but would love support this baby? Second thoughts consumed me; I didn't complete high school, didn't have a job, and I had no thoughts for the future. What was I doing? Though I was pregnant, that did not stop me from partying. I did not think once to stop any of my addictions of alcohol, marijuana, and cigarettes. I found out my prostitute friend, Nina, was pregnant too so I had someone to talk with during this time. She stopped using heroin and cleaned up really well, so much so that her parents let her stay with them. Nina would pick me up and we would spend hours just talking about being pregnant. I finally felt like I had meaning, some sense of purpose. This baby wouldn't be mistreated like I was.

At five months pregnant I still hung out in the streets, I met a guy who I thought really liked me. He would come see me almost every day. I didn't gain much weight during my pregnancy; I barley had a baby bump at this time. He still hung around when I told him I was pregnant. He was a heavy drinker so we would get drunk and hang out on Belle Isle—a park located in downtown Detroit. I met his brother but none of his other family members. He told me it was because they were prejudiced. I believed him, although the truth would come out soon enough.

At seven months pregnant, I made a decision to give the baby up for adoption. I forgot about the night I cried out to God for a baby so I could be loved. One of the things that became a reality to me was when my dad asked me how I was going to pay for the baby's delivery. I had no health insurance, so what would I do when the day came to deliver? This new question reinforced my decision to give up the baby. When we got to the Catholic Social Service office to begin the process, they told me about a home for teenage girls outside of the city. This place was a haven for pregnant girls who wanted to give up their children for adoption or needed a safe place during their pregnancy. While at the facility, medical insurance was made available to them through the state along with transportation to and from their doctor's appointments.

With that information, I signed the dotted line and off I went. It was weird when I got there because everyone talked so openly about their experiences and what they were going to do. Some girls had families selected for their babies. I felt very awkward since I was so late in my pregnancy and had just got there. I was giving my baby up for adoption, but wasn't sure if a family would take him or her. Would my child end up in foster care? I didn't know the sex of my baby yet since I hadn't been back to the doctor since my first visit at the free clinic. I was looking forward to finding out if I was having a girl or boy. My first appointment with the doctor was set and they took an ultrasound. When I found out I was having a boy, I was glad because I already had a name picked out. Even though I was giving up my baby for adoption, I still looked forward to naming him.

It didn't take long to get connected to someone at the girls' home. I met Cathy. She was a beautiful girl around my age who had a room right across from mine. Cathy and I became close; she confided in me and vice versa. Cathy's due date was a few months after mine, so we agreed to stay in contact even after I gave birth. My due date was August 8th which was after my birthday and meant that I'd be stuck in the girls' home celebrating rather than partying. I was finally turning 18 and would be considered an adult and I didn't want to spend it locked up somewhere, let alone sober. The girls would talk about different ways to induce labor. One of the tricks was to do sit-ups. They said doing sit-ups would cause the water to either leak or break. I had to try it, so on July 21st, I did sit ups before going to bed hoping to go into labor. I didn't have a problem doing sit-ups since I only gained about 11 pounds at that point in my pregnancy. My doctor's appointment was the next day so if my water broke or leaked, he could tell. Because I came so late in my pregnancy, a family had not been selected for my baby, but it was okay because I was sure someone would adopt him. The next day, the doctor confirmed that my water was leaking. So instead of going back to the girls' home, I was taken to the hospital. When I arrived, they had to give me something to induce labor since I wasn't experiencing contractions. After a few hours, the baby's heartbeat went down, but came back up after the contractions subsided. They placed something on the head of the baby to monitor the heartbeat more closely. I was not alone during this time because my labor coach and my dad were there. The girls' home assigned me a labor coach who would spend time with me during the pregnancy and would be my support system during the process. As we sat there talking for some time, the heartbeat went down again. This time all kinds of beeps came from the monitor and people came flying in the room. I was told to get on all fours and put the oxygen mask on. The doctor told me the baby was somehow losing air and the umbilical cord could be wrapped around his neck so they needed to do an emergency cesarean. After the surgery, the doctor confirmed that the cord was wrapped around the baby's neck not once but twice and he would not have survived if he went through the birth canal.

My first child was born weighing only 4 pounds and 11 ounces. I decided not to see the baby and was set on not connecting with him at all. The first time I stood up after the surgery was because I needed to go smoke a cigarette. We weren't allowed to smoke in our rooms so I had to go down to the first floor to the smoker's area. When I got to my feet, blood started gushing out of me creating a huge puddle on the floor. The poor nurse standing there holding me ended up with splattered blood on her uniform pants. It took a couple of people to clean me and the floor up, but afterward I still decided to go smoke. I managed to make my way to the smoker's area, but requested a wheelchair on the way back because I was in so much pain and could not walk back to my room. I talked the head nurse into letting me smoke in my room since no one else was in there with me. It didn't matter because in a few days I'd be out of the hospital and this would be nothing but a memory. When I had to fill out the birth certificate, I decided to leave the father's information blank. Why should I put his name down as father? If you asked me, he was only a sperm donor.

One day while the nurse came in to check my vitals, she asked if I'd seen the baby yet. When I told her no, she went on to say how he was the only baby left in the nursery and wouldn't stop crying. When she said that, I started to feel bad. She ended up convincing me to see the baby. When they brought him in, I saw this tiny little person wrapped so tightly in a blue blanket. I thought to myself, 'I can do this. I'll just feed him a few times and then just go home.' I kept the baby in my room and started feeding him. I wouldn't smoke when the baby was there and it seemed like he was spending a lot of time with me the few days I had left in the hospital. I began to keep every bottle that I fed him as a souvenir of my first born. The day the hospital released me was hard because I had to say goodbye to the little guy. I still took home the bottles I fed him.

I was going home empty-handed and free of any parental responsibility. I thought, 'Now I can go back to living it up just like before I got pregnant.' The baby had to stay in the hospital a few more days. He had gotten an infection so they had to complete the antibiotic regimen he was on, and then he would be released to foster care until a family was found. When I returned home and began to unpack my things, I placed each bottle on the table in the living room and found myself staring at them. That night I couldn't sleep, thoughts of the baby went through my mind. Why did I leave him? What if he's crying now and no one is there to pick him up?

I woke up the next morning and once again found myself sitting on the sofa in the living room staring at the bottles again. Suddenly I took my hand and moved it across the table knocking down each bottle and yelling out, "I want my baby!" I looked at my dad who came into the room to find out what was going on. I told him I didn't care what he thought because my baby belonged to me. My dad looked at me and told me that I would have to take care of him all by myself. I didn't care; I was going to get my baby. I quickly called the social worker at Catholic Social Services and she told me the baby was still at the hospital and I could go there and pick him up. She told me I had to sign more papers and then wished me the best as she hung up. I called my oldest brother and asked him to come and pick me up so I could get my baby. He came right away and drove me to the hospital. We couldn't get there fast enough. I signed the papers and grabbed my newborn son without taking into consideration the cost of being a parent.

It was difficult being 17 years old caring for a baby. My

father wasn't home much, so I had no support. My brother's girlfriend threw me a baby shower, which only a few people showed up to. The only people in my family that showed up were my father's sister and her daughter, who showered me with almost everything I needed. My brother's girlfriend was a great help to me. She would bring bags of clothes over for the baby and would take care of him during her time at the house. I think my son was lactose intolerant, but back then no one really knew why a baby would cry all the time other than being colicky. Looking back, I believe he was and life could have been much quieter. My poor baby suffered terribly, which made me a not so nice person. I started regretting the decision to keep the baby since he would not sleep at night because he was hungry and after having a bottle he would become very gassy. I was sleep deprived and did not like the idea that he totally relied upon me for care. I'm surprised he gained weight; it seemed like everything he ate ended up on my shirt. It wasn't until I put cereal in his bottle that he was able to hold it down and did not cry as much.

Shortly after the birth of my baby, my dad told me that he was moving and I could stay in the house. In theory it sounded great if I had a job or some sort of income to pay the bills, but I didn't. While in the girls' home, they helped me apply for assistance, which was only food stamps and medical. When I transitioned home with the baby, I was able to maintain the food stamps and medical assistance, but had no idea how to get any other benefits. When I called the social service worker, she tried her best to help me. She helped me get some money that I used to get things for the baby, but, of course, I had to supply my habits too. It was so hard. The bills kept coming in and there was not enough money to pay them. I got so angry at my dad for leaving me that I took it out on the gun cabinet he left behind. My grandfather made it for him and I knew it was special to my dad so it became the focus of my anger. I broke it up the best I could and made sure I called my dad to tell him about it. He was upset and I didn't care. That was the response I wanted from him. 'Hurt like me dad,' is what I thought. Someone needed to feel my pain. Why not him?

I kept in touch with Cathy and another young lady who stayed in the girls' home. When I told them I lived by myself they came by to hang with me. There were three of us sitting together in my living room talking about our relationship and money woes. We started talking about selling our bodies for money since the babies' daddies wouldn't give us any money. I thought what I did with Nina was only done by people who lived on the streets or did drugs. Well I was pretty close to living on the streets, so why not make some money? After all, most of the time I was giving myself away for nothing, I should get something out of it. So we came up with a plan. We asked another girl to babysit while the three of us went out. We came up with a code to protect each other since we didn't have anyone else looking out for us, like a pimp. One person stood watch and didn't go on any dates, using the buddy system to get the license plate of the car. We always used protection, absolutely no kissing on the lips, and didn't get into cars with any young guys. At the end of the night we split the money since the person who stood watch couldn't make money. Those were our rules. We also said when coming across someone who tried something outside of our rules to tell the others to avoid that person. I never went searching for someone to sell my body to so I relied upon the other two girls who had bragged about their experiences. The first night we made pretty good cash. I was the person who watched over the other two. It seemed pretty easy, but it was a whole different ballgame after the first night. I ran into some nice family men looking for something they weren't getting at home. Almost every trick we encountered wanted oral stimulation because that's what their wives wouldn't do. I ran into my old pimp friend, Mark, who offered his services since I was a street girl now, but I refused and told him it was only temporary. He told me Nina had gotten her act together since having the baby and didn't run the streets anymore. That was good to hear. I liked Nina and could tell that she was a good person just wanting to enjoy life. Mark gave me the scoop on a guy who was looking for companionship and would pay for it. That sounded like an easy task. When he introduced me to him, I was very surprised by his appearance. He was nicely dressed, clean shaven, drove a nice car and was very respectful to me. We went to get something to eat to talk about our arrangements. Through our conversation he revealed he had a family, held a well-paying job and was just looking for a companion. When we left the restaurant, he paid for the meal and then gave me some money for the time I spent talking with him. Our next meeting was scheduled and he said he would pick me up from my home so I wouldn't have to go in the streets to meet him. He said he wanted to be my regular date and would pay me enough so I wouldn't have to walk the streets again. He told me I was too pretty to do that to myself.

Our agreement was to meet once a week and get

something to eat and then go to the motel to spend time together. It was a great gig, since our time together had nothing to do with having sex, only talking. He would give me massages and tell me how much he appreciated talking with me. One thing he said to me that continues to ring in my head today was that he met with me because I gave him what his wife didn't, someone to talk to. He wanted to be heard as if he mattered. His job was stressful, his children were growing up and moving on so there was a hole in his life. I enjoyed our relationship. Heck, he was the only person I ever met that made me feel like I mattered.

It was cool to have this guy so I wouldn't have to sell my body anymore. I still went out to watch over the other girls, however one night it didn't turn out so well. I stayed home watching the kids because I was sick and Cathy had gone out with one of the girls to make some money. The sun was coming up and the girls still weren't back. The other girl returned and asked if Cathy had come home because she couldn't find her. I immediately became afraid because Cathy wasn't the kind of person to do something without communicating. I asked how they could have gotten separated. She began to tell me that Cathy told her she was going with a young guy and that was the last time she saw her. I began to wonder what to do. We were prostitutes and one of us was missing. Who would care? So all we could do was sit and wait, hoping she would show up.

Sometime before lunch the same day a cab pulled up and Cathy got out looking disheveled. We jumped up and opened the door to let her in bombarding her with questions. She told us what happened that night. She talked about how she got into a car with a young guy and he made a stop around the corner and a few other guys jumped in the car. She got raped and beaten by all of them and was told she was being transported to the place where they would kill her. She was in the back seat as they drove and as they were in motion, she reached over the front seat and grabbed the steering wheel hoping to hit something. It worked. They hit something and the police came and she told them the story. What I don't remember is if the guys were caught. Instead of being thankful she was alive we began with, "I told you…" not realizing how fragile she was. My heart was so calloused that instead of consoling her, I attacked her decision. In a way, I felt like she deserved it since she knew the boundaries. Cathy went upstairs to her room and we never talked about that incident again. From that day, we decided there would be no more street life for us. It was too dangerous and the reality of the dangers came through the front door that day.

It wasn't long after that I went into a dark place. I wasn't aware of postpartum depression, my baby was only a few months old and I began to feel like the world was closing in on me. It was like I was in a dream state during that time. Nothing seemed real. I hardly recall much of what went on except I felt like the walls were caving in on me and I wanted them to stop. I stayed high most of the time and don't even remember how I took care of my baby. I do remember one evening sitting on the sofa listening to music rocking back and forth. I wanted to be soothed as if the rocking would make me feel better. There were other times I would lock myself in a dark room and just sleep—me and my baby. One day I decided to call a friend who lived in another state. She said my baby and I could come and stay at her parent's house. When I broke the news to Cathy, she became angry with me since she wouldn't have a place to stay. I told her she could camp out at the house as long as she wanted, but I was leaving. I called my brother to offer him whatever was in the house. He came to get some furniture and while preparing to move an armoire, he discovered many empty bottles of MD 20/20, Wild Irish Rose, and other brands of alcohol in the bottom of it. I have no clue why was I saving those bottles but he placed them in the trash and never said a word. My decision to move out of state brought my mother back into my life. It was a relief to have her back, and though we didn't get along, she was still my mom. She told me to write as much as possible and she would keep in touch. Had I known doing something like that would have brought her around, I would have done it a long time ago. I may have acted like my mother wasn't important to me, but her approval meant a lot. I longed for a relationship with her, I just didn't know how to connect. I went to find myself an oasis in the home of my friend whose father was a pastor. I wondered if I'd find God living with them.

5
THE SURVIVALIST

When we left Detroit, my baby was four months old and it was the beginning of December. We moved to a southern state so I looked forward to a warmer winter. I was glad to get away and start over, a fresh beginning with just me and my baby. I'm not sure what I was expecting, but the family embraced us with open arms and welcomed us into their home as if it were our own. I was able to apply and get public assistance along with WIC, which helped supply baby formula and food. Life seemed to be pretty good for us there. The country atmosphere slowed me down and helped me feel more secure. I no longer felt like a dark cloud was over me. The family became a source of strength to me and to this day, I'm grateful for the open door they had for us. What I was not prepared for was seeing this family act very casual about God. I was expecting a household something like my aunt's, where there would be prayer meetings we would have to attend and Christian music would play throughout the house. I thought I would have to stop smoking and change my behavior when I moved in. That wasn't the case. The daughter and I began smoking weed together and one of their son's and I became intimately involved. I only saw the family pray together when the father would get ready to leave for Detroit after a short stay with the family. Don't get me wrong, they were good people who took me in and helped me regain my mind. However, I felt like if you gave your life to God then you would demonstrate a better way of living. That's the way I thought about Christians, but there was no difference between their family and mine except they went to church on Sundays. I found this family to be involved with infidelity, promiscuity, drugs, alcohol, and pornography. I felt no need to change my ways, but instead I fit right in.

The mother of the household was probably the greatest example of love. She allowed me to stay there and treated me like I was her own. I went to church with the family once on an Easter Sunday. They had to take me shopping for a dress because I didn't own one. It felt strange sitting there singing songs of worship and listening to my friend's father preach about a God whom I felt was very far from me. He preached about how Jesus rose from the grave and how great life was serving Him. I walked out the same way I came in, empty. I wanted something in life, but didn't know how to make anything good happen. I didn't know where to start. If I called on Jesus, would he help me? If he did help me, would I still remain the same? I always thought God wanted us to be holy because He is holy. It didn't help seeing this family function just as dysfunctional as me. They experienced pain, abuse, and perversion and their responses were just like mine. I watched them lash out at one another, using alcohol, sex, or drugs to relieve the pain of their own disappointments. What I didn't understand at the time was that they may have loved God, but were still ordinary people trying to work out their own issues the best way they could. They were just like me, struggling through life, except they had access to a hope of a better life. They held onto a belief system which could empower you to overcome the pain, but didn't utilize it. To me, it was worse than not believing at all. I didn't judge them since I believed they only lived out what they knew.

In the spring, my baby turned eight months old and I found myself missing my family I left behind. I appreciated the family who opened their home to me, but my heart was missing home. When I talked with my mom, I told her how much I missed everyone and how I wanted to come home. My mother missed me and wanted to help me get home, so she sent money for a bus ticket back to the city and we returned. I felt stronger and more together and I couldn't wait to get back home. Was I really ready for what was in store for me in the days ahead?

I arrived back in Detroit and found residence with my oldest brother and his girlfriend in a rough side of town. It was mid-April 1988 when I moved in with them. I was getting to know the people in the neighborhood and found a few girls to hang out with. I had my own little space in the back of the house. My baby and I slept on a mattress which took up most of the space in the room, but we managed. My brother's girlfriend cooked because I didn't know how. I wasn't very domestic; I barely knew how to use the washer correctly. I was able to give my baby his first birthday that summer. It wasn't a big thing, just cake and family. To me, that was more than enough. Since my son was able to walk, it made hanging out in the streets a little easier. He could walk with my friends and me.

In the middle of the summer, someone from Child Protective Services knocked on the door. The lady began to ask me a series of questions concerning my presence in the home. After responding to a few questions, I asked her what exactly was her reason for coming and she said there was a complaint that I was prostituting and taking my child with me. I couldn't believe it! When I was running the streets, no one said a thing. Now when it finally seems I'm straightening my life out, someone calls. I started thinking about who would have called them. Suddenly my mind flashed back to a run-in with my uncle who left his family and lived in the area. I asked the worker if it was him and she admitted it was and I told her that he was crazy and on drugs so his credibility wasn't so great. Nothing else came of the incident. I was told not to worry and she would dismiss the accusation. I told my dad about the incident and he was not happy since it was from someone who used to be married to his sister.

While staying with my brother, I got a job working midnights in a not so nice area. The girl across the street was the one who told me about the job. It was a place where we put together the weekly advertisements to be mailed. This job helped me make some money to buy diapers for my son. It helped me tremendously until my brother told me that he and his girlfriend were moving and I couldn't go with them. It had only been a few months and I was freaking out wondering what to do. Where would I go? Why didn't I ask my mom if I could move in with her? Our relationship was much better than before, but I don't remember if I asked and was denied or just felt like that wasn't an option based on historical responses.

On the plus side, I had become pretty good friends with the family across the street from my brother, maybe I could ask them. The family was nice enough to offer me a place to stay for $5 a month. It was a sweet deal at first, but after moving in, the realization of where I was makes my stomach turn to this day. The house was infested with roaches and it was disgusting. It was so infested with those critters that if you turned on a light in a dark room you could actually hear them as they scurried to hide somewhere. They had a drop ceiling in the dining room and the roaches would come out of little holes in the tiles. The kitchen was so full of them that no food was allowed to sit out and if you went into the refrigerator, you had to make sure to watch out because they would crawl in there. It was so nasty, but I was desperate and needed a place to stay so I had to suck it up. I still kept my midnight job, but I was forced to entrust my son with this family. It wasn't a smart thing, but when you're desperate you'll be amazed at what you subject yourself to. My poor baby was only slightly over a year old and didn't like being left with these people. I had no choice. I often cried when I prepared to leave because I knew they would put him in the bedroom where we slept and close the door leaving him in total darkness. I always put toilet paper in his ears before I left so he wouldn't have any roaches crawling in them. I hated where we were, but couldn't think of any other place to go. We would eat once a day and our menu consisted of box macaroni and cheese, hot dogs, or Cheerios. I didn't make much money and what I did bring home was enough to pay for diapers, cigarettes, bus fare, and food. One night while eating some macaroni and cheese something fell from the ceiling directly in front of me. When I looked down it was a roach that fell from the ceiling and dropped in my food. I was sick and threw the food into the garbage and made a decision to get the heck out of there.

I stayed with the family for about a month before running into another friend, Faith, who told me she had her own place. She told me I could move in as long as I could help pay half the rent. She said her aunt could help me get assistance with food stamps and medical care. In the meantime, I moved in with her with the hope to get public assistance and eventually my own place. I still worked a few nights while living with Faith who also had a child a little older than my son. She watched my son while I worked. This time I knew he was in a better place. For a minute, my life was finally making sense then I started to experience unusual bleeding in between my monthly cycles. I wasn't feeling well and since I didn't have insurance, I never went to the doctor to find out what was wrong with me. The good thing was it made me stop having casual sex. I took a couple of baths a day because I felt so dirty. I had to pass on what my friend Faith considered the most prized guys during this time. I didn't tell anyone what was going on with me; I just hoped it would go away soon.

One night my ride couldn't take me to work since he was upset I wouldn't put out, so I had to find another way to get there. Deciding to walk seemed to be the next best thing to do. I never took into consideration what could happen to me walking at night in a drug infested area, so I just opened the front door and left. While walking a few blocks from the house, I noticed a guy walking in the shadows behind me. Then it hit me, I have put myself in a dangerous position. I said a little prayer in my mind asking God to help me. As I rounded a corner, I noticed two white guys, who appeared to be intoxicated, walking down the street. I approached the guys asking them to walk with me because there was a guy following me. The guys were nice and said they would walk with me all the way to work. They had beer in their hand and offered me some. Usually I would drink, but I declined. I just wanted to get to work. We got high at work anyway so I decided to wait for my buzz until I was safely there. Just before reaching my place of employment the police pulled up. They talked with the guys and noticed that they were intoxicated. Since I had to get to work, I asked the policemen if I could go since they were walking me to work. They let me go and I made it to work in one piece that night. I never walked to work again after that night. In fact, if I didn't have a ride either by bus or cab, I didn't make it in.

My stay with my friend Faith didn't last long. Somehow the furnace went out and we ended up sleeping in our winter coats. It was the middle of winter and we were freezing. I found out Faith kept a heater in her room with the door shut and didn't bother to share that information. I began to think that maybe it was not the best place for my baby and I. I took a shot at asking my dad if I could come and stay with him and his girlfriend, Jennifer. By that time, I was in communication with the both of them and we seemed to have built a pretty good relationship. I was given the welcome mat to their home on the west side of Detroit and was relieved to get out of the frigid, two-family flat we stayed in with Faith. This would make our fifth move in one year. We lived out of garbage bags for the most part. We never stayed anywhere long enough to unpack our belongings. Regardless of where we went, no place felt like home. The more we moved, the smaller our bags became. Sometimes I would forget them at somebody's home or things would get taken. I didn't mind moving around; I was used to it. The problem was that I had this little guy with me who was feeling the effects of our moving around. My little boy was so clingy to me and I didn't know how to deal with it. I used to get so angry at him for wanting to be around me all the time, not realizing I was all he had. He kept me focused on making sure we had a roof over our heads and food to eat. There would be days when I wouldn't eat just to make sure he did. It felt good to be able to move in with my dad and Jennifer. I felt like our wandering days were coming to an end. It was a huge sigh of relief, but that sigh would become a sound of anguish.

6
CAN I JUST DIE NOW

When we moved in with my dad and Jennifer I felt like maybe I could breathe again. They lived in a nice home with her two sons and a couple of other relatives. There was no spare bedroom to move into, so our clothes were put in the basement and we slept on the living room floor. It was a lot better than sleeping on a mattress in a freezing cold house or a roach infested home. My dad helped me get on public assistance, since I wasn't able to get on it while living with Faith. I told my dad I had a job working midnights and asked him if he would be able to take me. He told me I would be better off quitting my job and applying for the assistance since it would be more money. I only worked a couple days a week which wasn't much when trying to save. The place where I needed to apply was not too far so I was able to walk to it. While applying for assistance I made the worker aware that I had worked part time, but was no longer working. She told me I needed to apply for unemployment and then based upon their response she would be able to open a case for me.

In order to get to the closest unemployment office I would have to take two buses to a side of town I wasn't familiar with. Jennifer was able to tell me which buses to take and handed me bus fare. On a cold February morning I entrusted the care of my son to whoever was at the house to watch him and left for the unemployment office. While walking to the bus stop a red car drove past me with a young guy behind the wheel. As I waited for the bus the red car pulled in front of me and the guy asked if I needed a ride and I kindly refused. As he pulled off I wondered if I made the wrong decision since it was cold and I wasn't sure when the bus would arrive. Fortunately, the bus pulled up a few minutes later and I got on. This is the first of two buses I would need to take in order to get where I had to go. As I got off the second bus near the unemployment office I was approached again by the guy in the red car. This guy was an attractive, clean cut looking black male with a nice car. Based on his appearance it didn't seem like he would have any problems getting a girl. I never once saw him as a threat. In fact, guys had approached me before and nothing ever happened so I didn't think it would be any different. I was flattered that he followed me all the way to the unemployment office. I didn't know any better. I was 19 years old and thought I was street smart, not realizing how naive I really was. I asked him why he followed me and his response was to make sure I got to where I was going safely. Being a white girl on that side of town alone made me a target, so he wanted to watch over me. What a bunch of crock which I bought hook, line, and sinker! As I went inside the unemployment office he parked the car and came in. He stood in line with me and struck up a conversation, telling me he lived just a few blocks from where he saw me and began asking me if I knew certain people in the neighborhood. He told me he would take me home instead of having to wait for the bus again since he did live in the neighborhood. I had a dollar and ten cents in my pocket and thought I could buy a pack of cigarettes instead of using it for bus fare if he gave me a ride. It seemed like a win-win situation for me, so I told him he could take me home. With that being said, he said he would wait in his car until I was done. After spending most of the morning in the unemployment office, I was finally able to go home.

When I walked out of the building, I began to walk toward the bus stop. Suddenly I remembered the offer the guy gave me, but something in my mind was saying just take the bus. I listened to this voice before, however this time I didn't. Later on I would wish I had. I turned around and walked back to the parking lot where I believed the guy in the red car would be. He was there waiting so I tapped on the window and he unlocked the door and I got in. It was one of the worst decisions I ever made in my life. We went onto the freeway and drove for a while. I was not familiar with the area so I just thought he was taking me home. We got off the freeway and began to ride through the neighborhoods. Something didn't seem right so I asked him where we were going. His reply was he had to make a stop. Silly me, I had no idea that he had other intentions in mind. We drove for about an hour and still didn't stop. I started feeling very uncomfortable. We pulled onto a residential street and parked, I stated something about knowing a person who lived on the block so he started the car back up and drove off. Finally my antennas were going up. I thought, 'Man, what in the world did I do?' The thoughts of my son at the house flooded my mind. My imagination began to go into overdrive at that point. I kept my cool knowing if I showed him panic I may not come out alive. We drove and parked on other streets and each time I would mention about knowing someone hoping he would just take me home. I was scared at this point since it had been over an hour since we left the unemployment office.

I started a conversation with him after noticing a joint in the ashtray. I asked if he got high. He said yes and lit up the joint and we smoked it. After smoking the joint we pulled up to a gas station and he asked me for my bus fare, so I gave it to him, so much for using the money toward cigarettes. Everything I planned had gone way out of my control and I was trying to find a way of escape. He locked me in the car and I swear I could not find the lever to unlock the door. I searched and pulled the handle hoping to just run out into the streets to get help. People were nearby, but not close enough for me to get their attention. My attempt to escape failed. He was on his way back to the car so I needed to act as if everything was alright.

Once again we drove for a few blocks then pulled into an alley. I was really nervous. He stopped the car and turned off the engine, grabbed my purse and threw it in the back seat. Suddenly, I felt something pressing against my neck. I didn't know what it was at the time but he began to sexually assault me. When he lowered his pants, I noticed he had toilet paper balled up in his underwear which at the time I didn't think much about it. In hindsight I realized that this was part of his preparation to clean himself afterward. I was so afraid; I didn't want to catch a disease. I hadn't caught anything from my previous encounters and I didn't want to get something this time. I remembered the condom in my purse (being told to always be prepared in the past helped me that day). He allowed me to get it and he put it on and as he began to rape me I heard voices of young children. We were parked at the edge of the alley where the sidewalk ended, so if anyone passed by they would see the car. I was so afraid. There were several times in my life where guys I knew would attempt to rape me, but each time I escaped from them. This time I wasn't able to escape the hands of a man I didn't know and had no idea what he would do with me after he was done. A million things ran through my mind. The first thing was my son. Who would take care of him if I didn't make it back home? I thought about the kids passing by on their way home from school, did they see us? Then my mind clicked into developing a strategy so that could I get out alive and get home. So when he was done, I looked at him and said, "If you wanted to have sex all you had to do was ask." I began to tell him how handsome he was and that I was sure he didn't have a problem getting sex from any girl. I asked him if he was going to give me his number so we could hook up again. He refused, but asked me for mine. I continued to say things that made him feel like the man—something I learned on the streets. If you want to get your way with a man, make him feel like he is king of the world. He threw the used condom into the alley and pulled up his pants. I was finally able to see what he pressed up against my neck—a screwdriver. In my mind, I grabbed the screwdriver and stabbed him a hundred times in his neck as I screamed at him, "How dare you do this to me?" I sat there in the passenger seat waiting to hear my fate. What would he do with me now that he's gotten what he wanted? He started the car and while backing out of the alley, he said he would take me home. I was relieved to hear him say that. I couldn't wait to get home to see my son. He dropped me off around the corner from where I lived and I ran to the house.

Trying to hold back the flood of emotions within me, I entered the house to tell everyone I was home. No one asked me what took me so long; no one really said anything to me. I left the house early that morning and it was around dinner time when I came back and I wasn't missed. I looked for my son, whom I found wearing what looked like the same diaper he had on when I left. It was so full of urine it almost touched the floor. I grabbed him and hugged him tightly. I was so happy to be able to hold my little boy again; it felt so good. After changing his diaper and realizing I hadn't eaten all day it made me wonder if anyone had fed him. I tried to go about the rest of the evening without saying anything. At the end of the day I tried to go to sleep, but I could only think of what life would have been like for my son had I not come home. Two days later I received a phone call. It was the guy who raped me. I had to give him my number that day. What if he pulled up to a pay phone and called to see if I gave the right number? I began to tremble as he asked if he could see me again. I do not remember what I told him since fear gripped me so tightly. The only thing I recall is hanging up and telling everyone, "If someone calls for me, I'm not here, ever!" I was shaking terribly. I couldn't keep it inside anymore. What if something happened to me? I was pretty close to one of Jennifer's sons so I asked him if

I could tell him something very personal. We went into the bathroom and I told him the guy who called me raped me the day I went to the unemployment office. I told him the whole story and asked him not to tell my dad. He told me I needed to tell my dad, so I did. It was hard for me to do, but I told him everything. My dad insisted that I tell the authorities and go to the hospital to have a rape kit processed. When I went to the police station, fear gripped me because I got into the car with this guy, why would they believe I was raped? Who gets in a car with someone they don't know and not expect anything bad to happen to them? I had to fix it, they had to believe me, and I didn't deserve to be raped. I couldn't unlock the door when we were at the gas station and felt trapped so I wanted this guy to get caught. After filing the report, I left with less weight on my shoulders. For the first time in my life, I told on someone who violated me. It felt good!

A week after the rape I decided to walk to the store for a pack of cigarettes. While walking to the store, I saw a red car driving down the block turning to a side street and stopping. I wasn't really paying attention to it at first until I got closer and saw the car and the person driving. It was him! He followed me as I left the store until he reached the street I lived on. I panicked and hurried to the house. Was this guy watching me? I was so afraid to step outside of the house after that. I told everyone when I ran into the house that the guy had followed me from the store. I was shaking. Should I report it to the police? I hadn't even heard from the detective, although I was told it would happen. I don't remember if I called the police or not. I was now confined to the house. It was February and nothing was going on anyway.

A few days after the incident, I asked if someone would walk to the store with me. A male relative of Jennifer made a joke by saying he wouldn't walk with me in the event the guy was bi-sexual. That would mean he'd go after him too. I was so angry with him for saying that and couldn't believe he would joke about something so serious. I was violated and he thought it was a joke. Jennifer's mother, who also lived in the house, asked what was meant when he said, "What if the guy is bi-sexual?" Full of fury from his remark and annoyed with Jennifer's mother because I believed she already knew what happened to me, the time bomb within me exploded. I went off on her, and said some things that I should not have even said. Everything that was pinned up inside of me was released in that moment. Unfortunately, it went toward Jennifer's mother, but at the time I didn't care. Why should I care? No one cared what was happening to me. I was slowly dying inside and the only thing that kept me alive was my son, but I didn't know if that was enough to keep me going. My life was falling apart and there was an innocent child relying on me. He was being mistreated by me and others because of my decisions. Had I given him up for adoption, he might not have experienced this type of pain. I was responsible for my child and was failing him miserably. That evening, my dad came to me and told me I had to move out because of what I said to Jennifer's mother. He told me he would give me all of the money I had saved with hopes I could get a place of my own soon. I couldn't believe what he said. This conversation reminded me of the time my dad told me he was moving out of the house we stayed in to live with Jennifer. Abandonment, rejection, and fear overwhelmed me as he walked away. My clothes were in the basement in garbage bags so packing wouldn't be a hard task. I was told to be out immediately. Who would take us in? We had no more options. This was the last place we had and now we would have to live on the streets. Where would we go? I was left to fend for myself and a little boy in the middle of winter with nowhere to go. I began to gather some of the things I had around the house and took them downstairs to put in the bags. My father came down, I don't remember why he did but it gave me a great opportunity to get some things off my chest. I was hurting and wanted him to feel my pain, so my words were not sugarcoated. I told him he was a terrible father and I no longer wanted anything to do with him. Why couldn't my dad see that I was hurting? For that fact, didn't anyone see the pain within me? Was my heart so cold and hard that its fragility wasn't showing? I cried that night wishing I could just die and avoid putting my son through any more trauma. Why won't I just die!!! As I lay on the living room floor tears streaming from my eyes, I hoped that I would just stop breathing so I wouldn't have to face another day of rejection and pain. I had to do something or we would be in the streets again, but this time we didn't have anywhere to turn for help. The night passed and as the morning sun began to rise I realized I had no other alternative.

I don't remember what time it was; I only recall that it was Sunday. I went into the kitchen to grab the bottle of Valium prescribed to me by the doctor who performed the rape kit. I filled a glass with water and went into the bathroom and closed the door. As I sat on the toilet seat reflecting on my life, tears began to fall from my eyes. I was hurting so deeply to the point of sobbing uncontrollably. I wanted to die and since it wouldn't happen naturally, I had to take action. I never seriously contemplated taking my own life before, but I felt like I had no other options. Though I held a bottle of alcohol to my mouth at times wanting to drink it and end my life, I would come to my senses and put it back down. I didn't think about writing a note explaining why I was going to take my life; there wasn't any time. I wanted to take the time to make a final plea to God. I wanted Him to forgive me because I felt like there was no alternative to my situation other than dying. I opened the pill bottle and poured a few pills in my hand and began crying out to God knowing there was no place else for me to go but Hell and I knew it. I began to tell God how sorry I was, but thought it would be better for my son if I died than live. I placed the pills in my mouth and took the water swallowing the first round without a problem. I knew my son would probably have a better life without me. I'm not sure how long I sat there begging God to forgive me and telling Him my life was terrible and asking why He allowed me to live when my life was full of pain. Why wouldn't He relieve me from the internal pain I was in and let me die? I took another handful of pills washing them down with another drink of water. I needed rescuing and I felt like no one, not even God, would do it. I didn't really want to die, but it was as if I had no choice. I remember getting up and looking into the mirror seeing myself for the last time, my eyes were swollen and red from crying. I wiped the tears and stared into the mirror hoping someone would come into the bathroom and tell me everything would be okay. I waited my whole life for someone to make me feel as if I mattered, unfortunately no one came. I then decided there was nothing else left to do but die. Sitting back down on the toilet to take the last of the Valium, I knew my life would soon come to an end. This was it, no turning back. I closed my eyes after swallowing the last of the pills.

Deep within me I felt a battle going on, a fight to live regardless of what was happening at the moment. I believe our bodies were created to live out its purpose on this earth and it fights to stay alive until we complete it. I don't remember getting up from the toilet seat, but I found myself in the hallway opening one of the bedroom doors and throwing the empty pill bottle at Jennifer's son. I recall him asking me what did I just throw at him and through my laughter responded, "I'm going to die." The next thing I recall is my father grabbing me asking what had I done as he placed me in a chair. Before the ambulance came, my son came to me and I hugged him and kissed him for what I thought would be the last time.

When I was placed into the ambulance the last thing I recall before blacking out was hearing a voice telling me I was in good hands now. It wasn't God or any of my family members. It was the EMT. I will never forget that moment because I felt as if that was the day I was being rescued. I woke up with something being shoved down my throat and hearing lots of voices around me. I wanted to stop this thing from being shoved down my throat so I clenched my teeth down on it. I started kicking and waving my arms around fighting with those who were trying to save my life. A woman's voice began to instruct me to stop fighting and allow her to get the tube down so it could get rid of all the poison I had just swallowed. She told me I would break my teeth if I continued to struggle. I was tired and couldn't fight anymore, so I opened my mouth and everything went black again.

I woke up with a tube still down my throat and someone telling me it would be a while longer so I could get some rest. I was still alive and now the reality of what I did began to hit me. I was left to my thoughts of hopelessness wondering what would happen next.

When they took the tubing out it felt like they were pulling my insides out. The remaining charcoal left in the tubing splattered on my gown along with some blood. I was able to sit up when the social worker came in. She asked me why I took the pills and I recall telling her, "To get attention." It just flew out of my mouth. I wanted to die to get someone's attention? What a way to get someone's attention, Lisa. Why didn't I just tell her that I didn't have anywhere to go? How about telling her I wanted to die in order for someone else to take care of my child? Why didn't I tell her that I had a small child at home and when I get out of the hospital we will be homeless? In retrospect, maybe it was a good thing I didn't tell her I had a young child at home; perhaps he would have been taken away. She asked me if I would be interested in spending three more days in the hospital for observation and evaluation. I told her I'd rather go home. I was released shortly after her visit. I'm surprised they let me go without committing me to observation since I had just tried to kill myself.

My father took me back to the house once I was released. We never talked about what happened. No one said a word to me when we returned. The decision to kick me out hadn't changed so I had to gather myself together and call my mom. When I called and told her everything, even the part about trying to kill myself, she said I could come and stay with her. She had my brother to pick me up since she was not a fan of my dad or of what just happened. I was a mess and needed to get my life together. My mom and I were finally on the same page to get my life together. She allowed me to move in and gave me the opportunity to save my money along with helping me look for a place of my own. My mom and I began to build a relationship during that time. I enjoyed my time with my mom. My younger brothers stayed with her also. I hadn't seen them for some time. I was still hurting but the reunion with them helped me to avoid dealing with the pain. I was never approached by anyone to get counseling for the rape or the suicide attempt. For years I lived in a state of not addressing what was happening to me, instead learning how to bury it deep within my soul. Sooner or later I would have to deal with it, but not now. Though my suicide attempt was not successful, I was still dying a little each day. My son began to enjoy having a stable home with people who loved and treated him well. After a few months I was able to save enough money to start looking for a place to live. I found a flat in Detroit, so with the help of my mother and her boyfriend I was able to move in with everything I needed. I was finally in a place where I could lay my head on a soft bed instead of a sofa or floor. It was during the end of spring in 1989 when I moved into my own place.

7
RESURRECTING WHAT WAS DEAD

I enjoyed having a place to call my own, there were no worries of being hungry or being put out because I did or said something wrong. Although I lived off of food stamps and public assistance, which also gave me health insurance for me and my son, I finally felt like I was able to breathe. I cooked and cleaned every day even though I didn't know how to cook. Some of our meals were undercooked and some ended up being extra crispy. I became friends with a single mom across the street who taught me how to cook. Though I got high with her and we talked about life, there were times when I would sit by myself and think about how life had to be much better than what I was experiencing. Although I was no longer homeless or wondering when we would get our next meal, there was a desire within me to do better.

One night while preparing to go to bed, I had thoughts about giving up cigarettes. I remember thinking about a time during the fifth grade I told one of the nuns at the Catholic School I attended how I wanted to be like her. There was something going on within me and I couldn't put my finger on it. Had I changed since the day I sat on the toilet and cried out to God? Did He hear me?

There was a couple with two teenaged children who lived across the street. Their teenage son would bounce a basketball in front of their house almost every day. My son, who was almost two at the time, loved to watch him play with the ball. One day while we sat on the porch watching the boy bounce the ball something kept nudging me to go ask if it would be okay for my son to play with him. As I walked toward the house, the boy turned and smiled at us. I asked him if his mother was home and if I could speak with her. When he came back outside behind him was a big woman who greeted me with a smile. She introduced herself to me as Linda. I asked her if it was okay for my little boy to play with her son and of course she had no problem with it. I didn't go home after that, instead we sat on her porch until the sun went down talking about life and children. Linda explained to me how she used to be a prostitute and her husband was her pimp until they gave their lives to Jesus. I was afraid to tell her anything about me except that I was a single mom. I remembered the man who led me to Jesus that one night when I was 16, however my life didn't turn out like hers. She asked if I wanted Jesus in my life and I told her yes. She led me through a prayer and gave me a Bible. She told me to start reading the Gospel of John. That night I went home and read the Bible she gave me. Was Jesus the change I was looking for? I wanted someone to take away all the pain and torment within me and according to her, Jesus was the one who could do it. That night I gave my whole heart to Jesus.

Something happened after that night. I no longer had a

desire to smoke marijuana or drink alcohol. I woke up the next morning feeling as if I was somebody. I was so excited to no longer have to count on drugs or alcohol to get me through the day. I knew Jesus would take it all away and I would be fine. The habit of smoking cigarettes remained, but I believed that would eventually go too. The excitement of my new conversion would soon wear off and the reality of walking as a believer would be tested.

Linda and her family invited me to the church they attended and offered to give me a ride. I accepted their invitation and was eager to meet people like her who accepted me for who I was. Getting up early on a Sunday morning was a hard thing to do since I was used to going to bed late and getting up just before noon. This church was nothing like the one I visited when I lived in the South. There was a live band and smiling greeters at the door who met me when I walked in. This world was new to me, people danced and lifted up their hands to worship the God I cried out to not long before. The nursery was available for children to stay while the parents could sit and listen to the preacher. Unfortunately my son would not let me leave him with anyone. Though he was very young, the scars of him being locked in a room were still there. I didn't understand it at the time and his attachment was frustrating me to no end. I never seemed to get a break. There was no way I could sit through service without having to leave due to his disruptive behavior and my inability to deal with it properly. Linda gave me what she thought was sound biblical advice concerning how to parent my son. Instead of spanking him with my hands, she suggested that I use a large plastic spoon on his bottom. She even used a scripture to validate what she said. Lacking the proper education in scripture, I took this for face value and began to use the "rod" to discipline my son. I didn't explain why he was being spanked or gave him a different behavior in place of the one he was displaying. He was just spanked, so it was almost like I was treating him more like an animal than a person. I didn't know of any classes available to help me properly parent my child and if there were any, I probably would not have gone. I actually believed I was doing what was right because this was what the Bible said, right?

Everything my son did made me angry and left me feeling like a failure as a mother and as an adult. It was like there was still this little girl inside of me fighting to be taken serious and still rendered powerless when my son wouldn't listen to me. I was my mother all over again. Just like she responded to me in anger, so did I to my son. I was not the safe place for him, just like she was not one for me. Was my son doomed to experience the abuse and pain I did? The vicious cycle of ignorance was being passed down to the next generation. I thought when you gave your life over to God and repented, everything would get better. Boy was I wrong, your history doesn't just disappear and you become this awesome person, there was a lot of work that needed to be done in me.

I was afraid people would find out about my past and consider me unfit to live for God. Every time there was a call for people to give their lives to the Lord, I would raise my hand and repeat the sinner's prayer over and over again. I felt dirty and ashamed and the comforts of alcohol and drugs were no longer there to ease my mind. There were nights I'd find myself sitting in a corner crying because of being tormented by the voices in my head telling me how worthless I was. The flashes of memories flooded my mind paralyzing me with shame and guilt for not saying anything. Rocking back and forth trying to comfort myself seemed useless since the voices in my head got louder and louder, only ceasing when I would beg God to help me. I struggled with my thoughts for months and was too afraid to tell anyone about them. This was the reason I took up drugs and alcohol in the first place, to drown out the thoughts which paralyzed me with feelings of hopelessness and emptiness. They were once silenced, but now there was nothing keeping them from shouting at me. I started smoking more cigarettes during this period. I had once again become a prisoner of my own thoughts.

I was afraid to let anyone in, though I went to church almost every Sunday and Wednesday. I would cry most Sundays after church because I felt so alone and that no one cared. The thoughts of worthlessness continued to plague my mind, keeping me imprisoned. How do I get out of this? How can someone like me become free? I know when I went to confession while attending Catholic school, I was told to do so many Hail Mary's and Our Father prayers in order to be forgiven. But what do I do now? The voices were screaming within me, but I felt like I needed to protect myself from being considered crazy, so I told no one. There were times someone would testify of their life journey, but I never heard anyone speak of having struggles with thoughts of worthlessness or how they felt less than a person. People only talked about how God blessed them instantly with healing, deliverance, or relationship issues. They used scriptures of how we are considered the head and not the tail, we are more than conquerors, and are victorious. Though these things are true, we can have a great end to a matter, but sometimes the road there may not be so pretty. I needed to hear about the journey not just the end result.

I never got up to testify of how God helped me stop doing drugs and alcohol since I still struggled with smoking cigarettes and so many other things. I started having sex with a guy who called himself a minister. He lived with Linda and her family. He made advances toward me one night while having a Bible study. I didn't refuse him since I was a new convert and still enjoyed having sex. He'd come over a few nights a week and we would have our rendezvous. We soon stopped after one night when I began to itch like crazy. He gave me crabs! He had been messing around with someone else and caught it from them and gave it to me. The next time I saw him, I called him out on it. Of course, he tried to lie, but he finally came clean. He told me he started having sex with another girl who had recently given her life to the Lord. Sound familiar? To top off this awkward moment, I told him I was pregnant. His response was he wanted a blood test because he didn't believe it was his. I became angry with myself for getting pregnant, but most of all I was upset to see a guy who called himself a minister acting no different than those on the streets. He responded the same way my son's father had.

The interesting thing about my pregnancy was that when I went to the doctor's office to confirm it, they told me the urine test came back negative. I hadn't missed my cycle yet, but I knew there was a baby in there. The doctor's office told me to come back a couple weeks after my expected cycle date, since it was too early to know. I went home and continued to live as usual. Around a week after going to the doctor's I began to experience severe stomach cramps and spotting. It wasn't like any of my regular cycles, so I asked Linda to watch my son while I went to emergency because perhaps this could be a miscarriage. Deep in my heart I did not want this baby and was hoping my body was rejecting it. Sure enough I miscarried. This was my third pregnancy and I'd just turned 20 years old in August, two months after giving my life to Jesus. After losing the baby, the voices in my mind became stronger. I not only killed one child but two. The condemnation I felt was overwhelming. I didn't have a voice to speak up and tell someone what I was going through, I remained in torment. The scriptures I taped on my mirrors and walls weren't enough anymore. I wanted help, but was afraid to admit my struggles. It was shame, not pride which kept me closed in. I had no idea how shame had made me so isolated, like a hermit afraid to get close to anyone. I kept people at an arm's length not because I wanted to but it was the only way I could protect myself from what people would think of me if they knew about my past. I really didn't know what a healthy relationship looked like; my whole life was spent protecting myself. To me, people could not be trusted. Being this way helped me survive in the streets. There were only small differences between my ways then and now. I may no longer swear, drink, do drugs, and sell my body, but my heart was still hard.

I finally went to the pastor of the church for help one Sunday after service and told him about some of my struggles. He asked me to make an appointment to meet with him during the week so we could talk more. While setting up the appointment with the secretary I made her aware of my transportation problem, and she assured me that someone would be able to bring me to the church for my sessions. Every appointment after that, someone from the church made sure I was able to get there and on time. I was excited to finally have someone who was interested to listen to my struggles and hopefully get what everyone else seemed to have—victory.

The pastor would send me home with scriptures and homework until our next session. One of my homework assignments was to read Chapter 4 from the Book of John, in particular the story of the woman at the well. I had to write a summary and bring it to my next appointment. This story was about a woman who influenced an entire town to come to Jesus because of Him telling her the truth about herself. When I wrote about her experience with Jesus, it was almost as if I regurgitated what the pastor said about the story in our meeting. Why wasn't I able to go any deeper than what was discussed in our meeting? I was a shell of a person unable to identify with my own feelings and not able to go deep within exploring my own heart to see how the woman at the well and I were similar. We both had encounters where the love of God superseded the pain of the life we were living. I didn't write in my paper how I was going around the neighborhood telling everyone about Jesus. I made cassette tapes of me talking about God's love to those who were in the streets and handed them out to guys who were trying to talk to me. I failed to mention how I approached prostitutes on the street telling them there was a better life available through Jesus. Instead, I just wrote whatever I heard the pastor say about this passage in the Bible. Still he saw something beyond the words of the paper. He saw me. When he handed my paper back to me, he wrote that God would use me to do great things regardless of my past. What a great thing to tell someone who felt worthless. Did I feel like God would use me like the woman at the well? I wanted Him to use me to do great things, but was I really worthy enough to be used?

In my last session with the pastor, he encouraged me to go back to school and get my high school diploma. He introduced me to one of the members of the church whom he thought would be a good help to me, a teacher named Lucy. She was an older lady whose children were currently in college so she became the greatest source of encouragement for me to get back in school. In 1990, three years after I would have actually graduated from high school, I enrolled in the adult education courses at the local high school in my neighborhood which also provided free childcare for students. I was on my way to actually getting my high school diploma, and this time I was determined not to quit.

My son was three when I started going back to school and since I didn't have a car at the time we walked. The school was about two miles from where we lived and my son was a trooper; he never whined or wanted to be carried during our walks. It was tough at times, because when it snowed I had to bundle him up in a snowsuit making his pace a little slower. I was finally feeling productive. I became friends with the two teachers who moonlighted as childcare providers. These two ladies took turns driving me and my son home during the winter months because they knew we walked two miles. I was finally finishing school and it felt great!

After about a year in school, I felt like getting a job

would help me even more. I didn't want to stay on public assistance for the rest of my life, so I wanted to take myself to the next level. One of the elders in the church gave me the greatest advice when interviewing for a job. He said, "In order for someone to believe in you, you have to believe in yourself." I needed to convince the person that I could do the job just as well or even better than a person who had experience. I took his advice and one day while at one of the local restaurants, there happened to be a help wanted sign in the window. Remembering what was said, I took the initiative to speak with the owner of the place and convinced him that I could do the job. The position was for a midnight shift waitress during the weekends. The owner said I could start that weekend and if I did well he would consider other shifts if I needed the money. I was so excited to finally have a chance to do something with myself. After a few months working as a waitress, I earned enough money to start saving. I opened my first savings account and each week I would deposit all the change I got from tips. The tellers weren't fans of receiving all those rolled up coins to count but I didn't care, I was saving for a car. There was another restaurant on 8 Mile Road which stayed open all night and they were looking for waitresses and this one had more customers which meant more money. I applied for the midnight position and got it. I was now making more money in tips which meant I could save more money and get a car quicker. I was able to deposit between $10-$15 a week instead of every two weeks.

There was one customer who came in every morning to get the same thing to eat before going to work. He was a nice older guy who always came in looking forward to talk to us about anything. One day near Christmas we talked about putting up the Christmas tree and hanging decorations. John (the customer) asked me if I had put up our tree yet. I told him that we didn't have a tree but that we would see one at my grandparent's house on Christmas. I don't recall John's response but the next day I got the shock of my life. The night started out with the normal flow of traffic at the restaurant which usually got slow at around 3:30 a.m. that's when we would begin cleaning the restaurant and prepare for the morning shift. As we sat together eating our "lunch," the manager and the cook asked me what I was getting my son for Christmas. I did not get any gifts for my son because I really wasn't used to celebrating anything anymore. I was grateful that my life seemed to have gotten better since I asked Jesus into my heart, but I still felt as if at any moment life could happen and I would end up on the streets again. I just told them I hadn't gone shopping yet. The next thing I knew the cook went into the back and came out with a bag full of wrapped gifts. I didn't think anything of it since I knew they weren't for me, but I was wrong. The manager told me how they overheard my conversation with John and decided to give me and my son some gifts for Christmas. I couldn't believe it. With tears streaming down my cheeks, I hugged them thanking them for such kindness. I remember going into the ladies' room shortly after we went back to work and began to thank God. There was a song I would play on the jukebox at the restaurant as I cleaned the tables, "A Place in This World" by Michael W. Smith. This song was my prayer and now I felt like God was finally convincing me that I did have value.

A few hours later during the same shift, John came in at his regular time and as usual I already had his order prepared to put in front of him. He was a nice guy and I learned that whenever you had regular customers who tipped as much as they pay for the meal, to make sure they had their food ASAP. As John was preparing to leave he said he was going on vacation so to make sure I enjoyed my holiday since I wouldn't see him until after the New Year. I told him Merry Christmas and to enjoy his time off. Before he left, he reached for my hand and placed something in it and closed it and told me to buy my son a tree and some gifts. I quickly ran into the ladies' room to see what he placed in my hand and when I opened it all I could do was cry. This man gave me a hundred dollar bill. Not only did I get blessed with gifts for my son and me, but I also had a hundred dollars. I cried in the ladies' room not once but twice that shift and this time they weren't tears of pain. That Christmas my son and I had a tree with decorations and presents underneath. Things were really looking up!

8
BINDING THE WOUNDS

By spring that following year, I started experiencing pains in my abdomen, pain so severe it would stop me dead in my tracks. One night lying in bed I began to press down on my abdomen searching for the reason why I was having this pain. On the left side of my abdomen I felt a large lump. I did not go to the doctor regularly so I didn't know what to do. The next day I asked my neighbor and she referred me to see her doctor and she assured me that he accepted the state assisted medical insurance I had. After undergoing several tests, the doctor told me I had a growth on my stomach muscle and he was not sure how it got there or if it was cancerous. He wanted to do surgery as soon as possible in order to have it tested and if any treatment was needed it would be done quickly. As the doctor was explaining this to me it was as if I was in a dream and after a while all I heard was an inaudible "wah, wah, wah, wah, wah." I couldn't have cancer; I was too young. I had my whole life ahead of me. I had a son and wondered who would take care of him if something happened to me. All those thoughts rushed through my mind as I went home. I recall getting into bed and crying out for God to heal me. I read in the Bible about Jesus healing the sick and lame. Couldn't He also heal me?

One night while watching television, Evangelist Benny Hinn came on and I began to cry as stories of healing were being told. I cried myself to sleep that night, I wanted all of this to end. Haven't I gone through enough in my life? I felt like my whole life had been nothing but a big struggle and here I was still having to fight. I was tired and deep in my heart I wanted to believe God was my only refuge from all of this. I just didn't know how it would play out. My job didn't provide any short-term disability so I would not get paid for the six-week healing process from the surgery. It was a good thing I was saving my money since my rent would still have to be paid and the only source of income was my waitress job. Besides being concerned about cancer, I also wondered who would keep my son while I was in the hospital and during my recovery time. I couldn't ask my brother and his wife since they had done so much for me already. I just hoped God would make a way through all of this.

As I worked one evening, a couple from the church came in to eat a late meal. The husband was an elder in the church and his wife was the most graceful woman I'd met in my life. Throughout the months I attended the church, the couple brought me clothes their son (who was a little older than mine) outgrew. I'm not talking about worn out clothing either; they gave him suits, sweaters, and pants that looked practically new. They were nice to my son and me, so when they came in the restaurant that night and sat in my section, I was happy to see them. I always worked the non-smoking section since all the other waitresses didn't want it. They thought church people didn't tip well and mostly those who sat in non-smoking were people who went to church. As I served this couple, they asked me who would be taking care of my son while I was in the hospital. I told them I still was working that out so I wasn't sure. They not only offered to keep my son while I was in the hospital, but also for the time it took me to heal. I was floored by their offer since no one knew my concerns but God and here they were asking to do the very thing I needed. They told me to think about it since I still didn't really know them, but to let them know if they could do anything for me during that time. That next morning as I walked home from work, I had an extra pep in my step. I felt like God was really concerned about me. A few months earlier I received money and gifts from people I barely knew which helped me start to believe in people again. Now, here was this couple offering to open their home to my son while I underwent surgery.

The final concern I had was school. I only needed a few more classes in order to graduate with my high school diploma and it was the middle of the semester and I was going to miss the last few weeks. Would I have to take these classes again and wait even longer for my diploma? I was a pretty good student and maintained a great GPA so when I went to class to inform my teachers I was in need of surgery and would be out the remainder of the year, I was told that they would make sure I had passing grades so that I didn't have to repeat those classes the next semester. I had to do extra work before I left in order to pass, but it was well worth it. My last concern was finally resolved. I felt better about the upcoming surgery. The fear of having cancer was no longer there; however, I still desired to be healed.

Our church held Sunday night services, which always featured a guest speaker. That night as the speaker gave his sermon, he asked if anyone was there in need of healing and of course I stood up and ran in line. This was the final thing on my plate. I wanted and believed in my healing! As I stood before this man with hopes to have him pray for me to be healed, something else came out of his mouth that shook me to the core. As I stood there with my eyes closed and hands raised high, he asked me if I was married, slowly opening my eyes, I looked at the man and replied, "No." He looked back at me and said, "Well, you will be soon, and what you see my wife doing (she was standing with her husband and prayed over the people who came for healing) you will do with your husband too." All I could do was close my eyes and say to God, "I surrender." As I walked back to my seat that evening I said nothing to anyone and after service I went home and cried. What no one knew was a few weeks earlier as I was praying I heard a voice say to me, "It's your season to be married." I knew it was God speaking to me, but marriage was something I did not want. Deep down inside I just wanted to be left alone because I was still dealing with the pain of my past. Who would want me? I had nothing to offer a man who really wanted to do something with his life. I was in school and had a waitress job, but I still struggled everyday to see myself any better than what I'd been through. I decided to just forget about what was said and focused on making my life better.

It was a struggle some days to get past the wounds of

rejection and abandonment from my youth. Being emotionally underdeveloped, it showed in the way I responded to people who awakened the feelings of insecurity. I would cut off all interaction with someone who reminded me of my insecurities. I gave people more control of my feelings than I gave myself. If something was said or done to me negatively and left me with a feeling of inferiority, I shut down and shut them out. Although I was in church, it didn't mean everyone was perfect, but because of my deficiencies I thought everyone was.

I remember one incident that left me pretty speechless. I would get a ride from one of the elders of the church who actually passed my house while in route to church. One Sunday after picking me up, the elder's wife asked me if I ever considered taking the bus. As I sat in the backseat of the vehicle feeling as if I was luggage instead of a person, I wondered how she could ask me this. She then began to talk about one of the church members who took the bus and how I should follow that example. I spoke up and reminded her that I had a child, while the person who took the bus was not a single parent. Regardless of that point, I reminded her that they passed my house on the way and did not realize it would become a big inconvenience for them to pick me up. Needless to say, I began to find other means of transportation to church after that. I thought, 'Wow! A leader in the church made me feel more like a burden rather than a person being an opportunity for ministry.' I did not think anyone in the church was obligated to pick me up, however, if she didn't want to pick me up anymore she could have just said so. This would not be the last negative experience, but it helped me realize that church people were regular people and had flaws just like me. Perhaps she thought she was empowering me and I took it as something negative. It's funny how we can hear words come from a person which end up becoming weapons of mass destruction because we filter them through our dysfunctional thinking. Heck, look at me, I professed God and I was full of shame, guilt, rejection and had a lot of bad habits to work through. I wasn't any better or worse than those who sat in the pews of the church. I lacked proper relationship skills because I hadn't experienced one that developed any roots, even within my family. I didn't get close to anyone, in fact, I ran from people. If an interaction with someone became more than an exchange of words, I froze. I did engage in conversations and social events, however, whenever it came to interactions going beyond the surface, I wasn't capable. I didn't know how to go deeper than "hello" and "how are you."

I tried to integrate with the other singles in the church by attending the singles ministry gatherings. At one of the gatherings we were asked to share who we were and what we felt God was calling us to. As each person began to speak about themselves and what God wanted them to do, I began to feel smaller and smaller because I really wasn't confident about who I was yet alone what God wanted me to do. Although I was back in high school, I also had a desire to go to college, but there was an internal struggle within me concerning what I would say when my turn came around. There was one person who caught my attention. Across the room sat a young guy who began sharing about the things on his heart. As he shared about the things he believed God put in him, all I could think about was how much I would like to have a guy like that. This guy knew what he wanted and I could feel the passion he had for God, and he was able to articulate the vision within him. The rest of the night was a blur to me because what I heard from this guy struck me and I wouldn't understand why until a few years later.

During the final months before my high school graduation I was asked to give a speech during the ceremony. The school set up a meeting for me to sit down with a couple of people to help put my speech together. I was graduating with honors and my life was looking great. When I met with the people who were helping me, they asked me to share some things about my journey in life up to that point. I began to share with them the struggles in my life and how everything changed when I gave my heart to Jesus. The writers became excited about my speech because they felt it would have a huge impact on graduation day. They were right, at graduation when I finished my speech I received a standing ovation. I was on cloud nine afterwards. I don't even remember walking across the stage as well as I recall the response from the speech. The only bad thing about it was when I placed the paper down to talk with people after the ceremony and came back to retrieve it, it was gone.

The best day of my academic journey had just taken place and became the catalyst for me to continue my education. I enrolled into the nearby community college, but needed to apply for financial aid, so one day at church I asked someone for help and they directed me to another member. When I approached the member for help, he told me I needed to talk to one of the young guys who actually worked in the financial aid office at Wayne State. The person he referred was the same guy, whom I'll call Mr. Confident, at the singles meeting who spoke confidently about the things God had placed in him. I wasted no time approaching him for help and he gave me his number to call him so we could go through the paperwork over the phone. I knew Mr. Confident was dating one of the single ladies in the church who I interacted with from time to time, so I appreciated his willingness to help me with no strings attached. I ended up receiving a reasonable amount of money for school and was excited because there was no other way for me to pay for school.

It wasn't long after submitting and receiving confirmation of my financial aid award notification that my phone rang and on the other end was Mr. Confident. He was checking to see if everything went well with my financial aid submission, so I told him I received money and was very appreciative of his help. He began to share some stories of working in the financial aid office so we talked back and forth about school, life, and God. I knew the girl he was dating and we talked about their relationship and what their future looked like. It wasn't long before we were talking several times a week for hours at a time. He was genuine and sincere which made it easy for me to talk with him. He became the brother I never had, one who could give you a male perspective on life. This was new to me since we never discussed anything inappropriately.

A few months after our friendship grew we attended a singles retreat hosted by another church. I was sharing a room with the girl I thought was his girlfriend, so there was hope in me to gain a better relationship with her. That weekend I learned through her they were no longer a couple. That was a shocker but explained why he hadn't mentioned her during our recent conversations. When I asked him about it he told me they had decided to part ways and felt it was God's will to do so. Our relationship continued to blossom and then one night changed everything!

He was the singles leader and there were times where we would go out as a group. He asked me if I would host a movie night at my place. I said yes and offered to cook dinner for the group. I already had the menu in mind: fried chicken, mashed potatoes, corn, and homemade biscuits. The movie night could not have come quicker. I worked midnights so after waking up that afternoon I began cooking up a storm. I was so excited to host something in my home and could not wait for people to taste my food. Mr. Confident came by a couple of hours before the expected time in the attempts to be a good host and he told me a couple of people called him to say they would not be attending the movie night. We were now expecting a smaller crowd than anticipated. The good thing was that I cooked enough food for the remaining people to have seconds. We left my place to pick up the movies for the evening and when we got back the remaining people called one after the other cancelling their attendance to the movie night. It ended up being me, my son, and this guy instead of the eight or so people enjoying the singles movie night at my place. After eating and watching the movies until midnight it was as if we didn't want the night to end, but would not admit it to each other. We began talking about life and the next thing I knew he began massaging my feet because I revealed to him how much they hurt after being on them all night at the restaurant.

His touch never went beyond my feet and for the first time in my life I felt like a guy cared for me without wanting to get into my pants. Before we knew it, it was 5:00 a.m. and he apologized for not keeping track of time since he felt it was not appropriate to stay overnight at a female's home. Watching him leave, it was as if a sudden rush of shame and guilt took over me. I actually enjoyed myself with someone of the opposite sex and felt like it was wrong. I thought since he had stayed so late at my house that we committed a sin, even though we didn't do anything but enjoy each other's company. Was I falling for this guy? Could I really have feelings toward someone? This evening awakened something in me and I did not know what to do.

When Sunday came and I went to church, I thought if someone looked at me they would know what happened even though no one was there but us. When he approached me that morning I began acting distant as if he didn't mean anything to me. I felt so ashamed to have enjoyed his company so much that I thought it was sinful. I knew he felt the coldness from me and probably wondered what in the world happened to me within the past 24 hours. For the first time in my life I was faced with something I had never felt before: How do I have a relationship with a guy without having sex? I started liking this guy and knew that if he didn't like me, I couldn't handle any more rejection in my life. Why did I feel so ashamed for liking someone who treated me with such care? On my way home from church all I could think about was this guy and how much fun we had being together. I was afraid to let him know that I was developing feelings for him for fear that he didn't have any feelings for me. Once he finds out about my past, he'd surely leave me alone. That evening my phone rang. It was him. There I was, trying to sort out new emotions, trying to understand me! How do I handle these inner contradictions? Why should it matter? I don't know how to have a real relationship without the strings of sex or drugs. Could this guy really want me in his life? Giving my life to Christ was the best decision I ever made. I know God loves me, is it time for me to learn someone else could too? My story doesn't end here…

RESCUE AND RELIEF

My story doesn't end here, but your life can have a new beginning. I've shared some intimate details of my life that once brought shame, guilt, and torment. Through the redemptive power of God I am no longer bound by the scars of my history. If you can identify with any part of my story and need relief from the pain. I invite you to open your heart and allow Christ in to bring healing, hope and a bright future. He did it for me he can do it for you! The Bible tells us we are saved when we confess with our mouth and believe with our heart that Jesus is Lord. I encourage you to pray this prayer:

Dear Heavenly Father, I repent of my sins. I believe in my heart that Jesus Christ died for my sins. I confess with my mouth that Jesus is Lord. With my heart, I believe that God raised Jesus from the dead. This very moment I accept Jesus Christ as my personal Savior. Amen.

For information about having Lisa speak at your women's ministry or church, to share how God used this book in your life, please contact her at:
P.O. Box 665
Farmington Hills, MI 48332
contact@inspirationcc.org

32171086R00062

Made in the USA
Charleston, SC
10 August 2014